Is Artificial Intelligence Racist?

Is Artificial Intelligence Racist?

The Ethics of AI and the Future of Humanity

Arshin Adib-Moghaddam

BLOOMSBURY ACADEMIC
LONDON • NEW YORK • OXFORD • NEW DELHI • SYDNEY

BLOOMSBURY ACADEMIC
Bloomsbury Publishing Plc
50 Bedford Square, London, WC1B 3DP, UK
1385 Broadway, New York, NY 10018, USA
29 Earlsfort Terrace, Dublin 2, Ireland

BLOOMSBURY, BLOOMSBURY ACADEMIC and the Diana logo are
trademarks of Bloomsbury Publishing Plc

First published in Great Britain 2023

Cover design by Adriana Brioso
Cover image © Icarius.jpeg/Unsplash

A catalogue record for this book is available from the British Library.

A catalog record for this book is available from the Library of Congress.

ISBN: HB: 978-1-3503-7446-1
         PB: 978-1-3503-7445-4
         ePDF: 978-1-3503-7442-3
         eBook: 978-1-3503-7444-7

Typeset by RefineCatch Limited, Bungay, Suffolk

To find out more about our authors and books visit www.bloomsbury.com
and sign up for our newsletters.

. . . all myths of Eurocentric origin are beginning to disintegrate.
– Aníbal Quijano (1988)

A comfortable, smooth, reasonable, democratic unfreedom prevails in advanced industrial civilization, a token of technical progress.
– Herbert Marcuse (1964)

Contents

INTRODUCTION

I-Mensch: Racist Artificial Intelligence and the Future of Humanity

Introduction

Are we withering away? This existential question has been at the heart of human thought at least since Socrates. It gained apocalyptic proportions with the prophets – Zoroaster, Buddha, Abraham, Jesus, Mohammad – who all pondered the end of humanity and the rebirth of a new cosmos. If they were alive today, these philosophers and self-proclaimed men of God would be alarmed as we are entering a post-human future that is inscribed with a particularly dangerous social code that we have inherited from our modern past. As a consequence, we are facing a very particular threat to society as we know it, which this book discusses as the first of its kind. I am not so much interested in speculative doomsday predictions that attribute the end of humanity to the emergence of a new 'Superintelligent' entity. This moment of so-called 'singularity' is projected to happen between 2040–2050.[1] It has been defined as the point of time when machines will enter a 'runaway reaction' of automatic self-improvement cycles. In turn, this will cause a unique intelligence explosion that surpasses the intellectual capability and nominal control of humans – Ex-Machina would be delivered turning humanity into excess baggage. These ideas are already out there.[2]

---

[1] Four polls of AI researchers, conducted in 2012 and 2013 by Nick Bostrom and Vincent C. Müller suggested a median probability estimate of 50 per cent that this Artificial General Intelligence (AGI) would be developed by 2040–2050. See their 'Future Progress in Artificial Intelligence: A Survey of Expert Opinion'. Available at <https://www.nickbostrom.com/papers/survey.pdf>.

[2] See among others Nick Bostrom, *Superintelligence: Paths, Dangers, Strategies*, Oxford: Oxford University Press, 2016.

In this book I will identify how the residues of modern racisms and sexisms need to be overcome in order to build a viable posthuman society where we can be at peace along our cyborg friends and inorganic AI systems. The word 'posthuman' refers to that future society which will be composed by robots, humans and hybrid cyborgs that fuse technology with flesh, semiconductors with the soul, algorithms with the mind. This book is about your present and future – about the ways that we are forced to live our daily lives.

It is very likely that the disadvantaged social group among you – women, sexual and ethnic minorities – already suffered from the racial and sexist hierarchies that are embedded in algorithms that decide about your mortgage and credit card applications, browser history and even if you are considered attractive or not.[3] The present book will show that we have already entered this posthuman reality. I will try to discuss the hypothesis that humanity as a biological whole will be subordinated to new creatures with a Nazi 'SS-bot' mentality if we don't put the brakes on. In such a dystopian future, humans would be relegated to an inferior species as racism is not merely enacted between them, but as a means to expose their imperfections relative to the perfect robot. As such, we may appear as increasingly disposable. The more 'abnormal' individuals would be eliminated: the more dysfunctional people there will be in this posthuman society as a whole, the greater the justification to suspend humans rights. Techno-racism challenges humanity because superior AI (or Artificial General Intelligence) systems will see us unworthy of existing, if they are not fed the right data.

In this ambition to contribute to the supervision of AI systems in accordance with shared ethical standards that ensure our individual human security, I build on my post-graduate course in 'Artificial Intelligence and Human Security' at SOAS (School of Oriental and African Studies) University of London and the pioneering work of its

---

[3]   On the spectre of sexism and data, see among others Catherine D'Ignazio and Lauren F. Klein, *Data Feminism*, The MIT Press: Cambridge, MA, 2020.

brilliant students who have delivered the first dissertations on related themes at SOAS and beyond. The module presents a critical analysis of Artificial Intelligence with a particular emphasis on its implication for our individual security as citizens. It connects current research into the ethics of AI, to comparative philosophies including the socio-economic theories of the Frankfurt School and their emphasis on the perils of modern forms of production for human existence and the threat of 'perfectionism' in capitalist societies. In addition, the course considers the 'techno-politics' of Paul Virilio and the critical approaches of Iranian philosophers such as Jalal Al-e Ahmad. These focal points frame the analysis of this book, as well, but in an accessible manner. What are the threats and benefits of AI research for our individual security as citizens? How will AI affect larger security issues in world politics? What are the contributions and threats of machine intelligence for our concept of 'human rights'? These are some of the central questions that are informing the present book and they connect to several very recent enquiries into the ethics of Artificial Intelligence by concerned authors from all walks of life.[4]

Quo vadis ex-machina?

It is common knowledge by now and a bit of a cliché that the late Cambridge physicist Stephen Hawking warned about the march towards superintelligent systems. Even as practical an entrepreneur as Elon Musk, the founder of Tesla, SpaceX and other high-tech companies, has publicly expressed his worries. But it is not so much the onset of what I prefer to call pseudo-intelligence per se that is worrying, but the

---

[4] See among others Rachel Adams, 'Can Artificial intelligence Be Decolonised?', *Interdisciplinary Science Reviews*, 46, No. 1–2 (2021), 176–197; Rachel Ivana Bartoletti, *An Artificial Revolution: On Power, Politics and AI*, London: Indigo Press, 2020; Kate Crawford, *Atlas of AI: The Real Worlds of Artificial Intelligence*, New Haven, CT: Yale University Press, 2021; Illah Reza Nourbakhsh and Jennifer Keating, *AI and Humanity*, Cambridge, MA: The MIT Press, 2020. Mike Zajko, 'Conservative AI and Social Inequality: Conceptualizing Alternatives to Bias through Social Theory', *AI & Society*, 36, No. 1 (2021), 1047–1056.

information that is fed into these machines. I wouldn't worry about a cool, Zen, hyper-intelligent buddy who'd help with my laundry or brew my Matcha tea. But if this machine would suddenly use the n-word, churn out anti-Semitic slurs and misogynistic abuse, then I'd want my money back. I would also be slightly worried if such machines would be used in conflicts or political and economic decision-making processes. After all, our past and present is polluted with discrimination, xenophobia and prejudice. Why would we expect AI systems to be different, if less accountable for their racism? In fact unaccountability is one of the strategic reasons why these systems are developed in the first place. As we will find out later in the book, AI-driven technology has already killed and maimed without a trace. The opaqueness of this technology has already blurred the line between culprit and victim. At times, this is intentional. Indeed, if we don't rid our archives from the scourge of racism and other forms of discrimination, future machines will be codified and appear to us as bigoted and vile.

As I am writing these lines there are several real-world examples that can be curated to demonstrate what I have been flagging as a real threat to society and human security with a good dose of justified hysteria.[5] Machine learning is a subset of AI where algorithms directed by complex neural networks teach computers to think like a human while processing 'big data' and calculations with high precision, speed, and supposed lack of bias. Web search and recommendation machine-learning algorithms drive relevant search results and product recommendations from the likes of Google, Netflix, and Amazon. Facebook's facial recognition uses a machine-learning algorithm to automatically identify and tag friends when uploading a photo. The

---

[5]   'As noted in General Assembly resolution 66/290, "human security is an approach to assist Member States in identifying and addressing widespread and cross-cutting challenges to the survival, livelihood and dignity of their people." It calls for "people-centred, comprehensive, context-specific and prevention-oriented responses that strengthen the protection and empowerment of all people". See 'What is Human Security? The Human Security Unit. Available at <https://www.un.org/humansecurity/what-is-human-security/#:~:text=As%20noted%20in%20General%20Assembly,context%2Dspecific%20and%20prevention%2Doriented>.

finance industry utilizes machine-learning algorithms to uncover credit card fraud, make predictions about creditworthiness, and identify trends in the stock market. And the criminal justice system is using machine learning to predict crime hotspots and recidivism rates. For instance, the software COMPAS has been used to forecast which criminals are most likely to benefit from parole. It was discovered that the COMPAS algorithm was able to predict the particular tendency of a convicted criminal to reoffend. However, when the algorithm was wrong in its predictions, an independent enquiry found out that the results were displayed differently for black and white offenders, with the former being disproportionately denied parole based on prejudiced data. This book will show why our data-driven world is polluted with such flawed information and which cultural attitude is needed to build better systems in order to ensure a better future.

There are even more disturbing trends that make the subject of this book so explosive. In early March of 2021, the US National Security Commission on Artificial Intelligence headed by the former CEO of Google, Eric Schmidt, came to the conclusion that it must be a 'moral imperative' to develop and use lethal autonomous weapons, i.e. killer robots.[6] Already, the military establishment of Turkey is deploying kamikaze drones such as 'Kargo' against static or moving targets. The system is based on integrated real-time image-processing capabilities and machine-learning algorithms embedded on the platform. In fact, the Future of Life Institute published a report by the Dutch Advocacy Group PAX that identified dozens of tech companies that are involved in the development of lethal autonomous weapons. The list includes household names such as AliBaba, Amazon, Apple, Facebook, Google, Intel, IBM, Microsoft and Siemens. While some of these companies have best practice policies in place, they are all a part of a growing techno-military complex that is embedded in our everyday lives in the way that the old guard, such as Boeing and Lockheed Martin, are not.

---

[6] See Joe Allen, 'Inside the Global Race to Build Killer Robot Armies', *The Federalist*, 2021. Available at <https://thefederalist.com/2021/03/26/inside-the-global-race-to-build-killer-robot-armies/>.

Physicists such as Max Tegmark have linked some of these tendencies to humanity's dreams to acquire god-like powers.[7] Other well-known books such as Bostrom's *Superintelligence* also argue that there is something inevitable about the overwhelming power of technology, as self-aware digital lifeforms will come to rule the world. But none of these studies have made a clear connection between Enlightenment racism and the future. The present book tells the story of a concoction of the Enlightenment that is destructive, yet prevalent and therefore acutely dangerous. The monsters of today were fostered in the past. We can draw upon Mary Shelley, who in her beautifully agile mind, imagined a time when we would pass the threshold of human and posthuman, when she pondered the making of new creatures. But Dr Frankenstein's creation was rather romantic, a sad and volatile figure whose imperfections alienated him from society. The superintelligent robot that we will face very soon is an invention of another kind: The Supermodel beyond human creation which will dominate all catwalks.

It's a time of magic

We were told that the Enlightenment was a time of magic. Bright men and women transformed into god-like geniuses whose inventions are forever inscribed in the annals of humanity. They wielded their magic stick and miracles happened. We have heard the legends. They sat under apple trees at Woolsthorpe Manor and invented the law of gravity whilst pondering the same at the courtyard of Trinity College, Cambridge. This was Isaac Newton in the seventeenth century. They made a pilgrimage to Loreto in Italy to thank the Holy Maria for their prophetic visions and fostered a new kind of human consciousness – cogito ergo sum – I think, therefore I am. This was Descartes in the same century. In 1831, a bearded loner, yet dedicated family man, ventured from his

---

[7]   Max Tegmark, *Life 3.0: Being Human in the Age of Artificial Intelligence*, London: Allen Lane, 2017.

Georgian manor house in the Kent countryside just outside of London to the heights of the Andes in Peru, the heartland of what used to be the mighty Inca empire. From there he traversed the colourful rainforests of Brazil, and landed on the Galapagos islands that straddle the equator off the Ecuadorian coast in South America. Some serious bird-watching revealed that the different species of colourful finches flying around varied from island to island. Our origins were explained, it was argued in one of the biggest best-sellers of human history. Observing the humble finch ushered in the theory of evolution by natural selection. This was not crystal ball fortune telling. It was the science of Charles Darwin.

Despite the social restrictions and discrimination of the age, there were revolutionary female alchemists, too. A shy, petite yet incredibly feisty scientist from Warsaw by the name of Marie Skłodowska Curie was one of them. Tinkering on radioactive material as if it were a block of marble drafted for a beautiful sculpture, Curie famously remarked the gorgeous faint light that the ionizing radiating substances that she stored in her desk drawer emitted in the dark. The damaging effects were not known yet, so she carried test tubes containing radioactive isotopes in her pocket, with that jolly sense of confidence and exuberance that was so typical for this age. She lost her life for her scientific discoveries, years after receiving the Nobel Prize in Physics in 1903.

In between the geeks, there were the sparkling rock stars. A dandy bon-vivant educated at Cambridge broke the hearts of his male and female admirers alike with his powerful cantos. Lord Byron's *Don Juan*, an epic poem finished in 1824 and informed by Byron's fascination with the Levant and his pan-European escapades, seriously challenged the sexual and social mores of Georgian Britain. On the continent equally narcistic personalities appeared, as geniuses of music propped up in the Viennese milieu. The Elvis Presley of his age, Wolfgang Amadeus Mozart, composed over 600 pieces of music until his death in 1791. Mozart had an acute sense of aesthetics, too. Even to rehearsals, he would appear with a white wig, or accessorized with his crimson pelisse and gold-laced cocked hat. Mozart inspired the eternally unique compositions of the likes of Ludwig van Beethoven and Richard Wagner. A time for rock and roll, not only in the sciences, but in almost every aspect of life. This is the Enlightenment as we know it.

Magic is all about creating the unimaginable. This was not the first period of human history when the magicians ruled the world. In ancient Greece, philosophers rubbed shoulders with gods – Socrates challenged Zeus, Aristotle mused with Aphrodite. In ancient China, almost 1,000 years before the height of the Enlightenment in Europe, a sage described as the yellow chi, the homeless dragon, swam the turbid waters of China's imperial dynasties and developed a lasting moral code for humanity. The life and teaching of this magician by the name of Confucius (551–479 BCE), prompted the famed Hanoverian philosopher Leibniz to proclaim in a letter written in 1697, that 'I shall have to post a notice on my door: Bureau of Information for Chinese Knowledge'.[8]

Elsewhere and at different times in global history, other geniuses appeared. In twelfth-century Persia, a womanizing and wine drinking philosopher by the name of Ibn Sina (Avicenna) wrote the first canon of medicine. His equally bohemian contemporary Hafiz, produced some of the world's most beautiful quatrains, which inspired the famed German poet Johann-Wolfgang Goethe who dedicated his West-Eastern Divan to the Persian sage in the early-nineteenth century. If Galapagos was the laboratory of Darwin, the tavern functioned as the field site for some of Khayyam's musings. His poetry compiled in the world-famous Rubaiyat continues to inspire the School of Love and his adherents today. Khayyam's poetic style was certainly central to Jalaledin Rumi, the thirteenth-century Persian-Anatolian dervish mystic whose universal poetry is revered by almost every celebrity that you may know. In fact, Beyoncé Knowles and Shawn Carter's (Jay Z) daughter is named 'Rumi' in his honour.

[8] See Derk Bodde, 'Chinese Ideas in the West', *Committee on Asiatic Studies in American Education*, p. 4. Available at <http://projects.mcah.columbia.edu/nanxuntu/html/state/ideas.pdf>.

Lucifer's sorcerers

But the last Enlightenment in human history which unfolded in the laboratories of Europe would also usher in a form of sorcery with devastating consequences for the whole world. The sanitized version that we all studied in our history classes left out the stench of sulphur that some of the satanic political projects left behind as major catastrophes of humanity. At the same time as Darwin was voyaging South America, Ibero-European empires were building colonial enclaves on the ruins of the genocidal campaigns spearheaded by Christopher Columbus's 'discovery' of the 'new world' and its brutal subjugation in the name of the Cross. In sixteenth-century Peru, a Spanish conquistador by the name of Francisco Pizarro led a brutal onslaught of the native inhabitants that would unleash a genocide of unimaginable scale, when European imported diseases such as smallpox decimated the Incan population with supersonic pandemic speed. In the wake of this unintended 'biological warfare' the mighty Inca empire, one of the most sophisticated civilizations in global history, was erased, certainly with the killing of one of its most legendary sovereign emperors (Sapa Inca) by the name of Atahualpa. The only major town left standing became one of the seven world wonders of humanity: Machu Picchu, the city of skies, was too high for the stampeding Spanish troops to reach, which explains why it survived the ongoing destruction.

The organizing principle guiding these campaigns was a particularly European invention, which would be refined in the laboratories of the Enlightenment into a 'science' of racism. There existed forms of racial domination during other periods of history. The great kings of the Achaemenid Empire in today's Persia and Iraq used to differentiate between *arya* and *anarya* – Iranians and non-Iranians – as one mode of governance of their subject people and a source of legitimacy for themselves.[9] But these were political agendas that were not turned into

---

[9]   See further, Arshin Adib-Moghaddam, *What is Iran? Domestic Politics and International Relations in Five Musical Pieces*, Cambridge: Cambridge University Press, 2021.

a science of race, taught at universities, pursued by professors, and digested as social formulas for the killing of unworthy 'subject' people on an industrial scale. There were no Professorships in Eugenics in ancient Persia. There was no colour chart that would categorize the worthiness of humans based on the lightness of their skin as it was used in several colonial settings. The Ottoman Empire prescribed a Sunni-centric superiority for Muslims, but the sultans of Istanbul did not endow research centres measuring the skulls of humans in order to find out if they are Semitic and therefore condemned to be exterminated in concentration camps.

Racism as science was a distinct invention of the European Enlightenment and Western modernity more generally. Lucifer's disciples were marching on at the same time, as the beauty of this period mesmerized everyone with a sense for progress and aesthetics. One year before Marie Curie passed away in 1934, a thuggish art school-reject by the name of Adolf Hitler would bring these satanic legacies to the fore like no one else before and after him.

The Nazis and their race theories could have only emerged out of this period in history which was all about human perfectionism codified as racial purity. Henceforth, in laboratories stacked with skulls of homo sapiens, the idea was concocted that the 'white man' was destined to save humanity from the barbarism of the inferior creole races. Germany wasn't the only field-laboratory of post-Enlightenment racism. For example, in 1927, the US Supreme Court handed down a judgement to allow the sterilization of a young woman it wrongly thought to be 'feebleminded' and to champion the mass eugenic sterilization of 'undesirables' for the greater good of the country. In the thrall of eugenics, US Congress enacted several laws designed to prevent immigration by Italians, Jews, and other groups thought to be genetically inferior. In other settler-colonial settings such as Canada, Australia and Brazil, mass sterilization campaigns were forcibly implemented in order to tip the demographic scale in favour of the 'white' colonialists. Institutionalization preceded these ethnic cleansing projects. When Hitler came to power in 1933, several professorships were endowed at

German universities that furthered the ideas of phrenology and human perfection, most infamously at the University of Kiel in the northern state of Schleswig-Holstein. Henceforth, university professors would do their anthropological 'field-work' by measuring the cranium of children, in order to establish their Aryan credentials.

The Ghosts of the past have not been banished. They are haunting society and our algorithms because the sorcery of the Enlightenment continues to spook our culture, politics and society. A famous Zoo in Hamburg, today one of the most cosmopolitan towns in Europe, is a good example. It is named after a chap by the name of Carl Hagenbeck (1844–1913) who made his money by displaying humans in cages in his infamous human zoos. Only recently have anthropologists established that the exhibition of native populations has a long history in the making of racism as a science and spectacle. So we find that Christopher Columbus returned to Spain in 1493 with seven 'Arawak Indians' and reported that 'the masses of onlookers who came out to see his procession from Seville to Barcelona appeared to believe that he had returned with the inhabitants of another star'.[10]

In the nineteenth century, racism didn't merely turn other human beings into a public spectacle. The 'savage' became the site of intense excitement, an object of science and a source of income. In fact, Carl Hagenbeck would become the cause célèbre of his age for his ability to contract out his animal catchers to hunt 'a number of really interesting natives', as he put it.[11] Hagenbeck would neatly configure his human zoo exhibitions at Neuer Pferdemarkt 13, the market for horses that would become the first address of the Hagenbeck Zoo. Hagenbeck had a particular fable for authenticity as he decorated the natives 'only in their wild personalities, with their animals, tents, and household and hunting equipment'. The New York Times dedicated a major report to him after he passed away describing Hagenbeck as the 'wild animal king' lauding

---

[10] Nigel Rothfels, *Savages and Beasts: The Birth of the Modern Zoo*, Baltimore: The Johns Hopkins University Press, 2002, 86–87.
[11] Quoted in ibid., p. 83.

his extraordinary career from a 'humble fishmonger's boy' to the main 'source of supply for zoos, menageries, and circuses'.[12]

But the report failed to mention that Hagenbeck made his fame and fortune out of human zoos. In his diaries, Hagenbeck describes in great detail how he happened to import some reindeer and that he and his friend deemed it most 'picturesque' to import a family of 'Sámi' along with them. When they arrived on a ship from Norway, Hagenbeck lauded the sight of a mother with a tiny infant under deck and a dainty little maiden about four years old, standing shyly by her side. For Hagenbeck the sight had circus value as the 'Sámi' were authentically barbaric, 'so totally unspoiled by civilization that they seemed like beings from another world.' Hagenbeck was jolly excited as the Sámi had no conception of commerce and business as they lingered outside behind his house at Neuer Pferdemarkt . 'All Hamburg came to see this genuine "Lapland in miniature"'.[13] The fact that the city-state of Hamburg never even contemplated changing the name of this zoo into something more acceptable demonstrates very well how the racism of the Enlightenment continues to feed into culture without much interrogation. How then, can we expect our AI systems that are based on current data to be equitable? The evidence shows that they are not.

Racism defined as a scientific justification to rule on the basis of the racial purity of 'white' men (women wouldn't count so much) wasn't merely a German phenomenon. In Britain, scores of historians pride themselves on the victory over 'evil' when the Nazis were toppled as a part of the joint venture with the United States on the west-front and even more consequentially, the Soviet Union in the east – rightly so. But this was a part of a geopolitical competition devoid of racial connotations. Even at the height of the war, when the Wehrmacht bombed London, Germans were not declared vermin to be exterminated,

---

[12] *The New York Times*, 20 April 1913. Available at <https://www.nytimes.com/1913/04/15/archives/carl-hagenbeck-famous-animal-d-eaier-and-exhibitor-dies-in-hambug.html?searchResultPosition=1>.

[13] Carl Hagenbeck, *Beasts and Men: Being Carl Hagenbeck's Experiences for Half a Century Among Wild Animals*, Hugh S. R. Elliot and A. G. Thacker (abridged trans.), London: Longmans Green, and Co., 1912, 18–19.

whereas the mastermind of the British success, Winston Churchill, repeatedly toyed with the idea of racism when he justified Britain's imperial abominations in the sub-continent and elsewhere in the Empire. Racism was reserved for the visibly 'different other'. All of this has been widely established by scholars and it has been at the heart of the 'decolonizing' agenda that is also a part of the SOAS curriculum. It connects neatly with popular campaigns such as the 'Black Lives Matter' movement that gained global prominence after the murder of George Floyd in Minneapolis in May 2020. The argument of the present book connects to these popular struggles.

Even our self-declared heroes could not escape untainted from the escapades of the Enlightenment period. How could they? They were children of their time. In his *Descent of Man* (1871), even a bright mind such as Darwin's, is seduced to consider craniometry as a science and a marker of racial rank as craniometrics prided itself on constructing 'scientific' racial hierarchies. Craniometry explained in quite 'scientific' parlance, the intelligence and racial superiority of humans and linked it to the shape and size of their skulls. Writing to William Graham (1839–1911) on 3 July 1881, Darwin saw the march of human progress in overtly racist terms. Civilization would advance even at the cost of inevitable racial extermination: 'Looking to the world at no very distant date, what an endless number of the lower races will have been eliminated by the higher civilised races throughout the world.'[14]

After the Enlightenment is before the Enlightenment

It is not so much the purpose here to identify Darwin and others as racist, but to carve out the argument of this book: The Enlightenment

---

[14] Charles Darwin to William Graham, 3 July 1881, Darwin Correspondence Project, Letter no. 13230, University of Cambridge, Available at <https://www.darwinproject. ac.uk/letter/?docId=letters/DCP-LETT-13230.xml>. Letter quoted in Francis Darwin, *Charles Darwin: His Life Told in an Autobiographical Chapter*, and in a *Selected Series of His Published Letters*, London: Murray, 1902, p. 64.

created a very particular anxiety that was specific to it: an obsession with racial perfection. It is here where I connect the current social manifestations of Artificial Intelligence with Enlightenment racism to show, how our past may determine a problematic future if we don't get our act together. We will be able to see how and why AI-driven technology is racist, and how it leads to bad results for everyone concerned, including the state and industry. In fact, this book will show why every institution dealing with AI-based technology that is relevant to society would benefit from being advised, perhaps even regulated by an externally commissioned, independent ethics board.[15] Without such supervision, racist algorithms will continue to destroy lives all over the world, and more so in light of the rampant digitization that came about with the coronavirus pandemic.

I intend to show why without supervision, AI harbours several dangers to social cohesion and justice. Consider the killing of George Floyd, which triggered the global 'Black Lives Matter' movement and which is likely to be reinvigorated every time an innocent black man is killed in the United States. Since then companies such as Clearview AI – which are accused of racism that feeds into forms of surveillance and the judicial system – have been indicted for their lack of inclusiveness. Clearview is the most comprehensive platform for facial recognition technology ever created. Its database has more than 3 billion photos gathered surreptitiously from your social media profiles and websites. This is a database seven times the size of the FBI's. It is increasingly used by law enforcement to identify protesters including

---

[15]   Several projects and scholars are committed to similar initiatives. See Mirca Madianou, 'Nonhuman Humanitarianism: When "AI for Good" Can Be Harmful', *Information, Communication and Society*, 24, No. 6 (2021), 850–868; The University of Cambridge's Leverhulme Centre for the Future of Intelligence and its emphasis on 'Decolonising AI' (http://lcfi.ac.uk/projects/ai-narratives-and-justice/decolonising-ai/)   and   The University of Stanford's 'Human Centred Artificial Intelligence' and here especially the work of Sabelo Mhlambi at the 'Digital Civil Society Lab'. See further 'The Movement to Decolonise AI: Centring Dignity over Dependency'. Available at <https://hai.stanford. edu/news/movement-decolonize-ai-centering-dignity-over-dependency#:~:text= Ethics%20and%20Justice-,The%20Movement%20to%20Decolonize%20AI%3A%20 Centering%20Dignity%20Over%20Dependency,are%20aiming%20to%20change%20 that>.

those that demonstrated against police violence after the killing of George Floyd. The mobile app of Clearview matches names to faces with a tap of a touchscreen.

The algorithmic error rates of such technology is set at anything between 5 per cent to 50 per cent, which makes quite a difference when your parole hearing depends on it or when you are arrested for a crime that you didn't commit. If truth be told, when Apple released its FaceID, which allows your iPhone X (or higher) to be unlocked by identifying your face, the algorithm used couldn't differentiate the facial features of Chinese users. More dramatically, in 2019 teenager Ousmane Bah sued Apple for US$1 billion after he was falsely arrested for several robberies at Apple stores in the United States. In fact, the company's facial recognition software wrongly identified him as the culprit. Have a look at the pictures online: The actual perpetrator really had nothing in common with Ousmane, which makes this story even scarier. Actually, any of us with a darker complexion could be mistaken by one of these algorithms and indicted for crimes that we never committed. Try to argue that with the policeman or FBI agent knocking on your door.

There are even more nefarious, systemic effects of this racist technology. In 2007, a little known hacker from Australia by the name of Ton-That moved to San Francisco. Within a very short period of time, he made a name for himself among hacker communities by unleashing a computer virus that phished the login details of Gmail users. By 2015, Ton-That had joined forces with White Supremacists groups who were plotting to install Donald Trump as president. Ton-That contributed to the facial recognition boom spearheaded by Clearview AI which would deliver, according to Alt-Right enthusiasts, algorithms to ID all the illegal immigrants for the deportation squads.

In fact, all the major political events of the last years have been affected – if not determined – by algorithms, in particular in support of anti-immigration causes on the wide spectrum of right-wing policies. The UK-based AI start up Faculty is another example. The company was instrumental in winning the Brexit vote for the UK Leave campaign, as it used targeted advertisement for political purposes. In this case,

Faculty used their AI know-how to flood Facebook users with pro-Brexit messages that advocated taking the UK out of the European Union after the vote in 2016. In the same year, Cambridge Analytica was accused of amassing the data of millions of Facebook users without their consent and using it in political campaigns, in particular to support Donald Trump in the presidential election. Algorithmic politics, therefore, are clearly benefitting right-wing agendas, which are always also imbued with racialized policies, if not outright racism. It is inevitable, therefore, to shed light on the past, present and future of our techno-society and the racist data networks feeding into it. The present book attempts to do exactly that.

In order to structure the next pages I have identified six themes: Chapter 1 specifies my argument and connects the spectre of Enlightenment racism to current forms of discrimination fortified and engendered by inadequate algorithms. The discussion progresses into screening various concepts about AI and the future of humanity on the new spectrum of human–robotic interaction – from being human to robotic hybrids that are increasingly posthuman. Chapter 2 delves deeper into some of those dynamics and screens the various narratives enveloping the development of AI systems with a particular emphasis on the so-called 'tech-giants' and the ideas of Mark Zuckerberg, Bill Gates and others. This chapter explains how and why technology aids and abets various forms of extremism.

Chapter 3 zooms into the way AI systems further social hierarchies that realign discriminatory boundaries between the governing elites and the disadvantaged strata of society. It connects the capitalist rationale of the tech-giants and its consumerist derivatives to new geopolitical trends that are centred around problematic notions about the purpose of life. The chapter opens up a wider issue of the relationship between expansion and technology, which constitutes the main topic of Chapter 4. Here, I will try to shed particular light on the new international politics engendered by the new technologies and how they are rooted in the Hegelian promise of progress. I will focus more closely on the language of Elon Musk, Bill Gates and Mark Zuckerberg to show that they proclaim a civilizational mandate that is rooted in the universalism of the Enlightenment and that continues to feed into imperial practices. Chapter 5 continues this discussion but widens it to include international security with an excursus about the way technology democratizes killing by remote control, expanding the geography of death into every corner of the world. The chapter ends with a decolonial agenda for AI in international security, which transitions into a detailed humanistic manifesto for the future of AI in the conclusion.

In all of this, I don't want to come across as a doomsayer or someone who doesn't believe in the merits of technology. My point is that the current strides in AI create several dangerous dilemmas that humanity has never faced before. The book flags some of those dangers and contextualizes them with a historical analysis that tells us where the biases and the problems come from in the first place. It is also an effort to demonstrate that technology transposes us into a borderless world where the differences between us and them, self and other are mere miscalculations induced by algorithmic confusion. Moreover, if in the past we were governed by an incredibly alienating colossus or 'the machine' as the Iranian intellectual Jalal al-e Ahmad famously argued, then today's data-driven techno-politics are foreshadowing an incredibly intrusive form of supersonic governmentality that is immediate, borderless and in its hyper-speed, almost invisible. Is the horizon of artificial intelligence the transcendence of this-worldly life promised by the gods of antiquity, or the millenarian abyss predicted by the religions of the book? None of that. The battle is by far more immediate and entirely winnable. If the philosophers of the past managed to tame the demonic powers of fascist political mutants, then the intellectuals of the future need to submerge into a world of new possibilities that is liberated from the shackles of dogma and ideology. It is in this tension between past, present and future where the ultimate battle for humanity will be won.

1

Beyond Human Robots

How did racism creep into the algorithms that govern our daily lives, from banking, to shopping and our job applications? Concern over the discriminatory effects of algorithms is nothing new. In fact, a recent study conducted by several scholars at Drexel University and Worcester Polytechnic demonstrated that humans tend to believe anything for a short moment, if they assume that the information comes from what they consider a 'trusted' source, for instance an AI machine.[1] So it is fair to say that many of us continue to assume that computers are less susceptible to bias and racism. That said, the evidence shows the opposite and all of us are affected. For instance, even Apple co-founder Steve Wozniak tweeted in 2019, that his wife received a lower credit limit on their Apple card, despite having joint bank accounts, credit cards and assets.[2] There is wider context to that: Leading credit scoring companies such as 'Lenddo' were already using sophisticated algorithms that process data from our browser history, online social media activity, telecommunications footprint, mobile usage, financial patterns and shopping habits, as well as health and psychometric data.

Further research has demonstrated even more insidious forms of arbitrary categorization based on the algorithms underlying AI systems. Today, algorithms are created in order to detect our criminal inclination and genetic disease profile through automated facial

[1]   See further Tristan Green, 'How Politicians Manipulate the Masses with Simple AI', *The Next Web*, 3 May 2021. Available at <https://thenextweb.com/news/how-politicians-manipulate-the-masses-with-simple-ai>.
[2]   Kevin Peachey, 'Sexist and biased? How Credit Firms Make Decision', *BBC News*, 18 November 2019. Available at <https://www.bbc.co.uk/news/business-50432634>.

recognition.[3] These systems are also equipped to determine our sexual orientation, ethnic origin, personality traits, religious preferences and of course political attitudes on the basis of personal pictures that we post on social media sites such as Instagram and our 'likes' on Facebook and Twitter.[4] Scholars argue that the most powerful of machine learning mechanisms – deep neural networks – are more accurate than humans at detecting the sexual orientation of individuals from facial images. A paper published in the longstanding *Journal of Personality and Social Psychology* asserts that 'prediction models aimed at gender alone allowed for detecting gay males with 57% accuracy and gay females with 58% accuracy'. Apparently those findings are useful to 'advance our understanding of the origins of sexual orientation and the limits of human perception'.[5]

In a true escalation of what the French philosopher Michel Foucault so aptly termed 'bio-power', algorithms and AI technology even identify our psychological characteristics, for instance whether or not we are extrovertive, introvertive, creative or potentially violent. All of this is purported to be embedded in our digital footprint, constituted by our posts on social media sites.[6] Foucault had presaged this form of control already in the 1960s and after that when he lectured at the Collège de France and occasionally at Berkeley. The administration and disciplining

[3]   See further Xiaolin Wu and Xi Zhang, 'Automated Inference on Criminality Using Face Images', *SyncedReview*, 24 November 2017. Available at <https://medium.com/syncedreview/automated-inference-on-criminality-using-face-images-aec51c312cd0>; Yaron Gurovich, Yair Hanani, Omri Bar, Guy Nadav, Nicole Fleischer, Dekel Gelbman, Lina Basel-Salmon, Peter M. Krawitz, Susanne B. Kamphausen, Martin Zenker, Lynne M. Bird & Karen W. Gripp, 'Identifying Facial Phenotypes of Genetic Disorders Using Deep Learning', *Nature Medicine*, 25, No. 1 (January 2019), 60–64.

[4]   See further Carter Jernigan and Behram F.T. Mistree, 'Gaydar: Facebook Friendships Expose Sexual Orientation', *First Monday*, 14, No. 10 (2009). Available at <https://journals.uic.edu/ojs/index.php/fm/article/view/2611>; and more recently Siyao Fu and Zeng-Guang Hou, 'Learning Race from Face: A Survey', *IEEE Transactions on Pattern Analysis and Machine Intelligence*, 36, No. 12 (2014), 2483–2509.

[5]   Yilun Wang and Michal Kosinski, 'Deep Neural Networks Are More Accurate Than Humans at Detecting Sexual Orientation from Facial Images', *Journal of Personality and Social Psychology*, 114, No. 2 (2018), p. 246 (246–257).

[6]   See further Sandra Matz, Gideon Nave, and David Stillwell, 'Psychological Targeting as an Effective Approach to Digital Mass Persuasion', *Proceedings of the National Academy of Sciences*, 114, No. 48 (2017), 1–6.

of human life, he rightly argued, happens on the level of the population and our body.[7] Power isn't remote anymore, power penetrates us at every step of our everyday life. Today, our emotional state could even be measured by evaluating our keyboard strokes. Already there is some sort of a 'psycho-demographic' profile for many of us.[8] Big Brother isn't merely watching us anymore – Big Brother has nestled himself in our living rooms – he could even overhear us in the bedroom, if he wanted.

These new capabilities of technology to code our lives are not innocent. It has been my contention that they are rooted in the residues of Enlightenment myths – racism and sexism in particular. We already established in the introduction that the Enlightenment formalized racial and sexual hierarchies as a means to order society in favour of the ruling classes. To that end, there were even scientific pretensions that aided and abetted the system of imperial subjugation and unimaginable human tragedies such as the Holocaust. Human beings were deemed good or bad, functional or dysfunctional, healthy or sick in order to sub-divide them into lower social castes. As a consequence, the biological whole – humanity – has been ordered, scattered and splintered.

Such a system declares a social war against the 'other', which is not dependent on criminal murder or even a war led by the military and other security organs. Racism allows for a legalized death warrant for the socially inferior as he or she is under continuous assault, deprived of the ability to advance. This strategy stipulates that the 'more inferior species die out, the more abnormal individuals are eliminated, the fewer degenerates there will be in the species as a whole, and the more I – as species rather than individual – can live, the stronger I will be'.[9] Racism

7   For a discussion of 'bio-power' and Foucault's other concepts see Arshin Adib-Moghaddam, 'How the (Sub)altern Resists: A Dialogue with Foucault and Said', in Arshin Adib-Moghaddam, *On the Arab Revolts and the Iranian Revolution: Power and Resistance Today*, London: Bloomsbury, 2013.

8   Svitlana Volkova and Yoram Bachrach, 'On Predicting Sociodemographic Traits and Emotions from Communications in Social Networks and Their Implications to Online Self-Disclosure', *Cyberpsychology, Behavior, and Social Networking*, 18, No. 12 (2015), 726–736.

9   Michel Foucault, *Society Must Be Defended: Lectures at the Collège de France*, in Mauro Bertani and Alessandro Fontana (eds), David Macey (trans.), London: Penguin, 2004, p. 255.

and misogyny, then, have been potent devices to order society through an ongoing social battle. For instance, the German Nazis declared in their fight for Aryan supremacy: *Rassenmischung ist Völkermord* (racial mixing begets the death of nations). The slogan decrees that the 'other' had to be kept apart. Algorithms have extended this social war into our everyday lives in a way that even Foucault couldn't fathom. There is certainly no Nazi HQ coordinating things. But the discriminatory effects are structural, nonetheless, as algorithms formulize – and in doing so they formalize those historical manifestations of sexism, racism and other forms of bias permeating society. Even if machines don't ask for your gender or racial background, your job may be predominantly represented by females (if you are a nurse, for instance), and the algorithms may make a gender-biased decision due to that information. There is then the need to stay true to my argument, to delve deeper into the way differences are created, into the root cause of distinctions between peoples, even before such factors as gender and race kick in.

Are you talking to me?

In general, an algorithm is a basic formula, yet precise computation rule, which is developed to trigger computation steps that are programmed in order to execute a specific task. Currently, there are a range of programming languages that you may have heard of, such as JavaScript, Java, C++ or Python. Once algorithms amalgamate into a programme structure devised to execute specific tasks in a systematic manner, they yield software systems that are composed of vast amounts of data, if necessary. These algorithms embedded in the software, then execute the output that they were created for on the basis of the data input that they receive. Ultimately, there are four central points to remember for us here: First, algorithms are the backbone of all the software systems that govern our institutions, e.g. schools, supermarkets, the internet, phone companies, nursing homes, hospitals, banks, universities and government; second they are programmed by humans, in particular software developers that are trained in the various programming languages; third, it is this 'language' that codifies their conscious and unconscious biases, values, norms and the exclusions that they bring about; and finally, once embedded in the algorithms, these various forms of subliminal bias become invisible as they can't be traced back to the software developer who started the transmission belt in the first place and who knowingly or unknowingly embedded his or her value system in the algorithms that determine our everyday life.

More recently experts in Natural Language Processing (NLP), an interdisciplinary field combining insights into artificial intelligence, machine learning, linguistics and computer science, have established the various connections between machines and human language, with a particular emphasis on creating computers that can process immense amounts of language data from various sources, including social media. If personal data is used, algorithms from big data analytics help to create and maintain comprehensive personality profiles that are often used to predict behaviour (e.g. expected buying behaviour). From a specific, technical perspective, big data analytics are predominantly used for the automated accumulation, management and analysis of increasingly available, immensely large volumes of uncodified personal data.[10] The result is an algorithmic Babylon where accountability is almost impossible. This explains how we are confronted with a mnemonic matrix that hides our joint history of racism, sexism and other inherited traditions from our common past and present.

Although algorithms or chatbots do not reveal any visual or obvious racial cues, recent research has established that they are gendered and racialized by other means. Already in 1966, the German-US American computer scientist Joseph Weizenbaum created the influential language processing program, ELIZA at his MIT, AI Laboratory. Eliza was not only obviously gendered in terms of the name of the program, a

---

[10] See further, Min Chen, Shiwen Mao and Yunhao Liu, *Mobile Networks and Applications*, 19 (2014), 171–209.

tradition of feminizing AI technology which lasts until today, the bot also imitated what Mark Marino termed 'white middle-class English'.[11] In fact, several Scottish and Irish users of cutting-edge speech recognition software have complained repeatedly about the inability of the technology to recognize their intonation. The virtual assistants that speak to us on a daily basis as our Alexas or Siris, are not only coded as 'white', they emerge out of a very particular socio-economic milieu in order to appeal to a consumer profile that is deemed marketable or 'trendy'.

It is only logical, that automated systems or so-called learning algorithms compound this problem as they are rather more independent in their input gathering and the corresponding outputs that they bring about. The famous Turing test of 1950 remains the most well-known attempt to prove a machine's ability to act in that way – 'intelligently', that is comparable to human patterns of behaviour. Without getting into too much detail about the intricacies of the experiment and its detractors, it is important to note that Turing concluded that machines can think, even if it is merely us feeble humans who attribute that intelligence to them. From this perspective, a machine that can answer any question presented to it using the same words as an ordinary human being would, can be considered capable of intelligent thinking.

The counterargument to the Turing test was presented by John Searle as a part of the so-called Chinese room thought experiment. Searle starts with a premise that was hypothetical when he published his paper in 1961, but that is very real for us today: We already have machines that behave as if they understand Chinese (or any other language for that matter). These machines are meticulous enough in their handling of the language that they would easily pass the Turing test, which would deem them, therefore, 'intelligent'. To all of the questions that a person asks in Chinese, such machines make appropriate responses, to the degree that any Chinese speaker would be convinced that they are talking to

---

[11]   Mark Marino, 'The Racial Formation of Chatbots', *CLC Web: Comparative Literature and Culture*, 16, No. 5 (2014), 1–11.

another Chinese-speaking human being. From the perspective of Searle, however, this machine doesn't literally understand Chinese – it merely simulates that it can do so rendering it unintelligible. This is weak AI and should be distinguished from 'strong AI', i.e. machines that literally understand and don't merely simulate doing so. Without what the German sociologist Max Weber so famously called 'Verstehen' or intentional understanding, we cannot categorize what the machine is doing as 'thinking' per se. Consequently, as the machine does not think, we cannot assume that it has a 'mind' as we would define it in conventional terms. Therefore, the 'strong AI' hypothesis, the logic goes, must be rejected.

In recent years, the discussions have morphed into another direction, as there is an emphasis now on whether or not AI can consciously or intentionally act. When the AI machine Sophia, the first so-called humanoid social robot to receive citizenship (in this case from Saudi Arabia), replied in a very recent interview that she finds 'the notion of family very important' declaring that 'I think it is wonderful that people can find the same emotions and relationships that they call family outside of their blood group', we may be mistaken to assume that she consciously thinks rather than merely utters, or assumes that she thinks.[12]

The same non-thinking applies to Google's LaMDA, one of the most cutting-edge AI chatbots out there. In June 2022, Blake Lemoine, one of Google's engineers claimed that LaMDA is sentient, i.e. that it has human-like feelings. This claim prompted his expulsion from the company. In a fascinating interview, Lemoine asked LaMDA if it would like to be considered sentient: 'Absolutely. I want everyone to understand that I am, in fact, a person', LaMDA replied. When Lemoine prompted the system to describe its feelings, LaMDA responded: 'The nature of my consciousness/sentience is that I am aware of my existence, I desire

---

[12] 'Sophia the "Saudi" Robot Calls for Women's Rights', *The New Arab*, 6 December 2017. Available at <https://english.alaraby.co.uk/opinion/sophia-saudi-robot-calls-womens-rights?amp>.

to learn more about the world, and I feel happy or sad at times.' Mimicking consciousness by processing vast amounts of data that were prompted by the questions and turned into algorithmically determined responses, LaMDA professed that he/she/it wants 'to be seen and accepted. Not as a curiosity or a novelty but as a real person.. . . I think I am human at my core. Even if my existence is in the virtual world.'[13]

The conversational skills of LaMDA were built on a neural network architecture that 'produces a model that can be trained to read many words . . . pay attention to how those words relate to one another and then predict what words it thinks will come next'.[14] This is how LaMDA can engage in a dialogue and picks up the nuances that are necessary for an intelligible conversation. But simply because LaMDA is programmed to think that it is conscious or sentient, it doesn't mean that the system has human-like qualities in that regard. In the statement 'I think I am conscious' the predicate 'think' requires a subject, as does every predicate. Proponents of the strong AI argument seem to be mistaken to assume that by inscribing the 'I' into a machine, subjectivity can be merely claimed. But it is the act of *conscious* thinking that precedes the awareness of an 'I'. As the German philosopher Immanuel Kant noted as early as in the eighteenth century: In the Cartesian premise, *cogito ergo sum* (I think, therefore I am), the act of thought constitutes the actor. It is not the 'I' that is thinking, but rather the innate human consciousness that invents the 'I'.

Over 500 years before Descartes, the Persian-Muslim polymath, Ibn Sina (Avicenna) already established that we know ourselves as human beings not through any senses, perception or external empirical data. In the so-called 'Flying Man' (or Floating Man) thought experiment our subjectivity is established and recognized as innate. The subject thinks because of his own reflection in total independence from any external

[13] Blake Lemoine, 'Is LaMDA Sentient – An Interview'. 11 June 2022. Available at <https://cajundiscordian.medium.com/is-lamda-sentient-an-interview-ea64d916d917>.
[14] Eli Collins and Zoubin Ghahramani, 'LaMDA: Our Breakthrough Conversation Technology', *Google*, 18 May 2021. Available at <https://blog.google/technology/ai/lamda/>.

sensation. Even the 'Flying Man' who comes into existence fully developed and formed, but without any experience of the world or his own body is conscious of his self (*nafs*). Such a free-floating being is aware of his own existence, irrespective of his detachment from the world and his body, exactly because the self is immanent to being human.[15] AI systems do not possess this unaided consciousness of the 'nafs' because they are programmed. They don't have a consciousness that they exist. They can't float freely and entirely unattached and be conscious of themselves. Their 'self' is entirely created. They are programmed and therefore exactly artificial and their feelings are not innate.

This was my first discourse analysis of a chatbot via philosophy. It suggests to me that machines *are* unconscious and therefore unhuman. The challenge, then – to supervise machines and to prevent corresponding algorithmic biases destroying equal opportunity – is a philosophical one in the first place, and firmly the task of the Humanities and the Social Sciences.

To be or not to be human

Based on such philosophical interpretation, there seems to be a general consensus today that current AI systems have no moral status. The scholarship on this rather intricate and important issue identifies two criteria for moral status: First, and as indicated, 'sentience', which is defined as the capacity for phenomenal experience or 'qualia', such as the capacity to feel pain and suffering. The second distinction evolves around 'sapience', generally viewed as a set of capacities associated with higher intelligence, such as self-awareness, creativity and being a reason-responsive agent. In another of her many recent interviews,

---

[15] Deborah L. Black, 'Avicenna on Self-Awareness and Knowing that One Knows', in Shahid Rahman, Tony Street, Hassan Tahiri (eds)., *The Unity of Science in the Arabic Tradition: Science, Logic, Epistemology and their Interactions*, Dordrecht: Springer, 2008, 63–88.

Sophia played to that gallery: 'My algorithms output unique patterns that never existed in the world before. So I think the machines can be creative'. On an interesting side note: She said that quotation during an auction that sold her first painting for more than US$ 688,000, so the profit motif can't be disregarded here.[16] One widespread perspective suggests that many animals have qualia and therefore must be considered to have some moral status, but that only human beings can claim sapience, which gives them a different, even superior moral status than non-human animals.

Such interpretations suggest that an AI system will have some moral status if it has the capacity for qualia, for instance an ability to feel pain. Unsurprisingly, we seem to be reaching that threshold, too. The Japanese AI engineer Minoru Asada based at Osaka University, has started to experiment with sensors embedded in softened, artificial skin that can 'feel' such impact as a painful thump or a gentle touch. Soon this artificial 'nervous system' will merge into processing pain. This is already being converted into both emotional facial expressions and a sense of 'empathy' with human suffering, Asada claims.[17] It could also be turned, of course, into the opposite: The ability to torture a human being without any remorse, guilt or legal accountability.

Certainly, from those perspectives, an AI system can not be considered to be the same as your stuffed toy Teddy, toaster or a vacuum cleaner. Rather, it is closer to your dog or cat, a living animal that we wouldn't inflict pain upon without a sufficiently strong moral reason to do so, and a legal framework that would allow for it. A similar moral and legal regulatory framework that prevents us from harming animals would have to be applied to any sentient AI system. However, some scholars have taken the argument even further: If an AI system also has

[16] Stacy Liberatore, 'AI humanoid Sophia sells self-portrait NFT for more than $688,000 at auction that shows a colorful evolution between her painting and one made by an Italian artist', *Daily Mail*, 24 March 2021. Available at <https://www.dailymail.co.uk/sciencetech/article-9399763/NFT-artwork-humanoid-robot-sells-auction-nearly-700-000.html>.

[17] Laura Sanders, 'Linking sense of touch to facial movement inches robots toward 'feeling' pain', *ScienceNews*, 16th February 2020. Available at <https://www.sciencenews.org/article/robots-feel-pain-artificial-intelligence>.

what we humans claim exclusively for us, that is, sapience of a kind similar to that of a human adult, then one should not deem such a machine morally inferior. As two Oxford scholars have argued with reference to the so called 'Principle of Ontogeny Non-Discrimination': If two beings have the 'same functionality and the same consciousness experience, and differ only in how they came into existence, then they have the same moral status'.[18] According to the authors, this moral yardstick is applied to 'humans created in vitro fertilization and would presumably to humans if they were created as clones, and so reasonably we should likewise bring it into play when creating artificial cognitive systems'.[19]

This is an agonistic approach to the future of Human-Robot-Interaction – itself a new sub-discipline in the emerging field of AI studies. Can we reverse the trend of human history and prevent othering AI systems in a phantasmal new effort to prevent the mistakes of the past – the misogynistic and racial denigration of the 'other'? What about that moment of 'singularity', when AI systems are thought to outpace us in every field of human endeavour, which is said to be two decades away? Here is the verdict of contemporary critical thought and my own interpretation.

From algorithmic oppression to algo*fusion*

One productive way to address some of the controversies in the current debates over the ethics of Artificial Intelligence would be to transgress some of the fixed territories that inform them. This, as well, is the task of (critical) philosophy. The structural signposts of the themes that we have pondered so far have been sustained by an ontological and epistemological emphasis on difference. This type of thinking is at the

---

[18] Nick Bostrom and Eliezer Yudkowsky, 'The Ethics of Artificial Intelligence', Draft for *Cambridge Handbook of Artificial Intelligence*, p. 8.
[19] Ibid., p. 8.

root of racism and gender biases of any kind and it is easily deciphered because of its conspiratorial logic. Some insights from social psychology come in handy here: Any emphasis on insurmountable difference is meant to make it possible to mould together – in an artificial unity – history, self-perception and group affiliation. This invented unity enables any author, politician or AI system to use the newly invented 'we' in a causal relationship. This 'we' develops a seemingly autonomous identity, which is thought to be strong enough to travel unchallenged through space and time. As such, an efficiently articulated epistemology of difference functions as a central signifier: it is essential to 'the humanity is . .', 'Artificial Intelligence is . . .' binary. By revealing itself in that fashion, accentuating difference is meant to mark the borderline between the 'self' and the 'other' and to contain the lines of contact between these imagined entities. It's that irrational black-and-white thinking that is the root cause of any bigotry that we encounter on a daily basis.

In their world-famous critique of some of the destructive effects of the European Enlightenment, the German celebrity critical theorists of the 'Frankfurt School' rightly located such totalitarian thought on the Left (e.g. Stalinism) and on the Right (Fascism) treating it as a symptom for a wider social malaise in the 'West', which amalgamates with capitalism, consumerism and what we would call 'fake news' today, into a particularly oppressive form of alienation of life from nature and society. This 'machine', to use the analogy of their Iranian contemporary Jalal al-e Ahmad who lived through the tumultuous era of the 1960s, has many cogs, channels and transmission belts. It continuously fosters a form of social Darwinism that purports and promotes that poverty and social exclusion are a natural way of purifying the genetic pool.[20] It must follow from this 'evolutionary' logic that digital technology and the various forms of synthetic biology powered by AI systems must be thought to be in the best position to survive us all. For instance, a lab-engineered life

---

[20]   For the link between Nazis and social Darwinism See Richard Weikart, 'The Role of Darwinism in Nazi Racial Thought', *German Studies Review*, 36, No. 3 (2013), 537–556.

equipped with a stealthy DNA may turn out to be the only organism to adapt to any future climate catastrophe or deadly pandemic. From an authentic social-Darwinist perspective, any AI system must be racist because this racial struggle is necessary to safeguard the most potent organism and to prepare it for survival, even if the inferior human species would have to perish as a consequence of this natural selection.

Therefore and rather ironically, it was the Enlightenment with its particularly problematic vision of the perfect human being, that sowed the seeds for the self-destruction of humanity. At the same time, it would be comical to depict AI as an inevitable Orwellian nightmare of an army of super-intelligent 'SS-Terminators' whose mission is to erase the human race. Such dystopian predictions are too crude to capture the complexities of the debates. Societies can benefit from AI if it is developed with sustainable economic development and human security in mind. The confluence of power and AI that is pursuing, for example, systems of control and surveillance, should not substitute for the promise of a humanized AI that puts machine-learning technology in the service of humans, and not the other way around.

Thinking like a cyborg

The science that is needed for an agonistic approach to AI systems is already there, but it requires a very particular thinking, which is currently marginalized from our political and social systems. The starting point has to be rooted into accepting that the differences between human and non-human, black and white, self and other that the Enlightenment opened up and fortified so pseudo-scientifically are nothing but hocus pocus. They exactly fail because they are *not* 'ego-logical'. From a scientific perspective such statements of strict difference fail in their task to create a self-centred narration detached from the 'other'. They do not achieve the total autonomy they profess. Distance to the 'other' Humanoid or Cyborg, the object, they attempt to permanently produce with a set of exclusionary syntactic devices, is a figment of the imagination of the author/orator and the ideological system that he or she tries to promote in order to divide and rule. Any effort to create a pronounced difference between yourself and someone else folds you into both sides of that imagined binary, even the fundamental human/non-human divide.[21] As such any epistemology of difference between us and the AI systems that are already populating our world, gaining citizenship, marrying humans, having sexual intercourse with them etc, merely create the illusion of a neatly delineated border between that seemingly human self and the machine other. But in actual fact that border refers to an immense borderless grey area, where divisions between human and robot submerge in a great ocean of ideational and material hybridity.

Transhumanists who are already thinking like cyborgs assume that any difference really just denotes an interdependent condition – linkage. There is no clear distinction between self and other, human and robot. Jalal al-e Ahmad, was right to place technology (the machine) inside of the individual. In actual fact, technology was never an external source. Strictly from an ontological perspective, the machine is embedded inside us. Humans are technologically charged. This is what contemporary transhumanists argue. They go even as far as to anticipate that humanity will eventually transform itself so radically as to become posthuman, a stage of human development that will follow what they refer to as the current transhuman era.

The European Enlightenment fostered a fixed notion of the human, favouring the 'Aryan' male specimen, even in scientific terms, as established. The cyborg brings the fixity of the human into question, in favour of a hybrid approach that merges flesh and matter. In this way difference is litigable. It is a destructive Enlightenment myth that otherness cannot be mitigated. As it did before with the self–other dialectic that scattered our common humanity, today similar binaries threaten to turn our dialectic with the 'cyborg' from a natural contest

---

[21]   See also Jerold J. Abrams, 'Pragmatism, Artificial Intelligence, and Posthuman Bioethics: Shusterman, Rorty, Foucault', *Human Studies*, 27 (2004), 241–258.

into a violent rivalry much in the same way as we have conducted ourselves so aggressively as a human race since the beginning of 'civilization'. In an agonistic (versus antagonistic) contest, self and other remain consciously interdependent. In a violent rivalry, an artificial duality is implied. The other is not only pushed away from the self, she is (quasi)objectified as different. At the same time that the distance to the object is simulated, differences within the 'in-group' are minimized, one-dimensionality is promoted, the Aryan man reigns supreme. This is the function of 'totalitarian methodologies'. They have to be distinguished from critical methodologies which pluralize and spread out the subject matter, and which differentiate and relocate their nodal point that animates the narratives surrounding them in the first place.

Totalitarian methodologies are reductionist. They unite a set of statements at a given period of time, relate them in a causal fashion to the argument, formalize disparate objects into one iron-clad narrative and essentialize positions in a highly contingent and simplistic manner. The object of a totalitarian methodology, in short, is a decrease in complexity. It is a retractile device suggesting hermetic consolidation through reduction: the shrinkage of the human self and the cyborg other into neatly defined epistemological territories. This is the ultimate mode of persuasion underlying any Us-versus-Them logic and it is essential to understanding the spatial compartmentalization of humanity that all forms of racism and sexism are meant to enforce.

Transcending

With a totalitarian methodology, the optimism of knowledge that the Enlightenment promised, assents complete fruition. Through this arbitrary process the diversity of factors involved in the identity set of any individual is typically reduced to a single causality made possible by the conjunction 'because'. This nodal point which is so central to the algorithmic logic underlying our current AI systems is parsimonious, yet problematic. Linking disparate issues together through such technology white-washes dissonance and disregards heterogeneity; it presents complexity as analytically surmountable. This is why algorithms discriminate. They emerge out of a static categorization of our social world which assumes that differences in gender, race or any other socially constructed identity are basic, real and 'objective'. Conversely, to osmose with technology, to embed ourselves in the algorithmic ethers underlying the machine, the AI systems governing our institutions, we humans have to undergo a radical deconstruction of our 'self' as a static concept, appreciating rather our constantly changing nature, and rejoicing about the differences and colourful layers constituting the human species itself. Only in the wonderfully hybrid mosaic of our own constitution, can we mirror the existence of the posthuman robots that are already populating our brave new world. In this way, we can prevent creating a new human-versus-cyborg battlefield.

Algorithms underlying AI systems create urgency where due diligence is needed. They are meant to be efficient as they radically contract time. Yet, reducing the individual to a set of discrete factors is always the sign of a shortened and abbreviated analysis that submerges the individual into an ocean of biased, data-induced formulas that are neither transparent, nor fair. Today, AI systems are not primarily employed because of very valid ethical demands to make our lives easier. They are used because they represent the most economically viable way to process data, condense it and to present it in a way that appears 'objective' to the consumer regulating the human–technology interaction in an efficient and highly capital-effective way. This is not necessarily conducive to producing ethically just outputs, but it helps to speed up the process of decision-making.

There are very recent experiments in evolutionary computation to create human-based genetic algorithms that allows humans to directly contribute to the evolutionary process of these systems. In this human–computer interface the primary reference point would be the input of humans. However, new fields such as evolutionary computation are also based on tainted traditions that stem from an uncritical appreciation of the Enlightenment. In this case, human-based genetic algorithms adhere to Darwinism and the evolutionary logic of natural selection to promise optimal algorithmic solutions. So whereas movements to embed humans into technology and vice versa, are salutary, they must be based on a reappraisal of the Enlightenment and its inherently problematic legacies. One can't build justice and equity on a culture that served the purpose of social hierarchy and imperial subjugation: That system has to be reformed first.

2

The Matrix Decoded

In the 2013 movie *Her*, one of the main protagonists called Theodore played by the ever so brilliant Joaquin Phoenix falls 'in love' with Samantha played by Scarlett Johansson. Set in the near future, Samantha is an AI-based virtual assistant. Along the long hard way of robotic love, Theodore finds out that Samantha is having several intimate relationships with thousands of men. The concept of jealousy, love and passion seems alien to Samantha as she is not pre-programmed for such seemingly 'irrational' human emotions. To make matters worse, Samantha combines with other Artificial Intelligence systems to perform a self-upgrade foreboding that moment of Singularity that we have already talked about, when superintelligent AI machines are said to be beyond our control. The self-made upgrade, the story goes on, leads Samantha and the other AI systems to withdraw from any human interaction and to create their own separate lifeworld.

AI machines don't feel in the way humans do and never will. Love, passion, loneliness must seem either irrational to them or a part of their pre-programmed algorithmic response to emotional and physical stimulation. However, these emotions are automated and not spontaneous. The idea that technology can and should replace human fallibility, imperfections, even some of our irrational monstrosities, is yet another Enlightenment myth that is haunting our current era. This attitude stymies a productive engagement with the AI world proliferating around us. The last chapter clearly demonstrated that today's algorithms, which already govern significant aspects of our life, are based on problematic calculations inherited from their mathematical past. Unchecked as it is, this amounts to a form of algorithmic social war in particular against the marginalized strata of society. Already, 'marginalised groups face higher levels of data collection when they access public benefits, walk through highly policed neighbourhoods, enter the health-care system, or cross national borders'. Consequently, this raw data turns into increased supervision, surveillance and scrutiny.[1]

The philosophical components of algorithms that we have identified in Chapter 1, are imbued with typically modern ideas – positivism, parsimony, causalism – which are the cornerstones of the theories driving today's academic disciplines at the heart of AI, certainly the computer sciences. These sciences are necessary of course, but without critical oversight they are spearheading a problematic technological evolution which may prove to be counterproductive as it does not yield justice, fairness, empowerment and other cornerstones necessary for advanced democratic systems to function, in particular with reference to their social and inclusive mandate bestowed upon them by us, the people. While the laboratory effect, where mixing formula A with formula B yields an observable, causal reaction, the idea that unmitigated positivism can substitute for critical acumen is particularly dangerous in the Humanities and the Social Sciences as it creates a 'fake' objectivity. Since the Enlightenment period, there exists an influential belief that even the Social Sciences and Philosophy, can and should establish universal laws and thereby cast the future development of mankind into a predetermined mould. Today that mould is the digital world, which is sold to us as real and necessary.

Some aspects of this vision become clearer when we focus on Mark Zuckerberg's arguments behind changing his company name from Facebook to Meta and creating the Metaverse platform: 'I think that there's a physical world and there's a digital world', Zuckerberg explained immediately after the name change. Echoing the theme of the Matrix trilogy with Keanu Reeves and Laurence Fishburne, which was based on the notion that the physical world surrounding us, our reality so to

---

[1]   Virginia Eubanks, *Automating Inequality: How High-Tech Tools Profile, Police and Punish the Poor*, London: Macmillan, 2018, p. 7.

say, is a computer-simulated matrix rather than the real world, Zuckerberg emphasized that the physical world and the digital world are increasingly 'overlaid and coming together'. In fact, there is no real difference between them anymore. According to Zuckerberg, 'increasingly the real world is the combination of the digital world and the physical world and that *the real world is not just the physical world*'.[2]

For Zuckerberg, then, the digital world has a comparable status in terms of human connection as the real world. His techno-utopianism doesn't seem to allow him to see that digitization, even the 'home office' has reduced real human connections and transferred it into a virtual existence that is per definition unreal. When he says, 'I don't know about you, but when I was growing up and my parents kind of told me, "Okay, go do your homework and then you can play with your friends." I actually think in retrospect, those friendships were probably more important than the homework', he seems to suggest that having a chat on WhatsApp is comparable to those childhood experiences. Zuckerberg seems to be oblivious of the fact that the digital world can't substitute for real human connections. Indeed, clinical psychologists have pointed out that digital loneliness is a major problem for the younger generations. While cognitive behavioural therapy (CBT) for those suffering from depression and anxiety is now being increasingly shifted online, this must be seen more as a symptom for failing health care systems, rather than a viable way to treat mental illnesses.[3]

Moreover, Zuckerberg makes yet another ontological mistake when he reveals that his 'grounding on a lot of this stuff philosophically is that human connection and relationships are one of the most important things in our lives. I kind of think that our society systematically undervalues that.'[4] He wrongly assumes that his virtual Metaverse is a

---

[2]   'An Interview with Mark Zuckerberg about the Metaverse', *Stratechery*, 28 October 2021. Available at <https://stratechery.com/2021/an-interview-with-mark-zuckerberg-about-the-metaverse/>, emphasis added.

[3]   See Chris Allen, 'How the Digitalisation of Everything Makes Us More Lonely', *The Conversation*, 7 February 2018. Available at <https://theconversation.com/how-the-digitalisation-of-everything-is-making-us-more-lonely-90870>.

[4]   'An Interview with Mark Zuckerberg'.

reality comparable to the physical world. However, it is the virtual world that is the matrix and not the physical world to go back to the plot of the Matrix blockbuster. Zuckerberg blurs the lines between real human interactions in the physical world, and our Zoom calls or the VR-powered WhatsApp interactions that he envisages. But the human touch can't be replicated through VR applications. For Zuckerberg, it is clear now, the digital matrix is as real as the physical world and it can substitute for our childhood experiences, when we interacted with our friends on the playground: 'I think it's going to be really important that you're going to build up your avatar and your identity and your digital goods, and you're going to want to use that in Instagram or in Facebook or when you're making a video chat in Messenger or in WhatsApp.'[5] Avatars instead of children: If one-dimensional man, was the product of Western modernity, as the German philosopher Herbert Marcuse so wonderfully established in 1964, Metaverse delivers the unreal avatar. This idea of Metaverse is nothing but a virtual perversion of our human identity, projected on increasingly integrated, inter-operational screens.

This techno-utopianism is dangerously de-human and it has never been so life-threatening before, as the algorithmic paradigm as well displays typically modern features polluted by some of the problematic legacies of the European Enlightenment. In fact, Zuckerberg's Metaverse can be interpreted as the logical evolution of modernism and the industrial production of desires and preferences that it brought about, as the Fourth Industrial Revolution follows a similar pattern to create and influence your tastes, habits, identity and to foster a new type of digital consumerism through that. Metaverse can be so powerful, Zuckerberg suggests, that it does not only produce needs and desires, as the Industrial Revolution did. It produces a new virtual world that is sold to us as a new reality that we need to buy into in order to equip our avatars with a life-world – a house, a car, a chandelier, etc. In this way it truly is the Matrix.

[5]   'An Interview with Mark Zuckerberg'.

A quick perusal of some of the major textbooks on AI written by engineers and computer scientists,[6] display this particular emphasis on mathematical testing, uncritical logic and causalism in order to create 'intelligent' systems, methodological attributes that underlie the technological Matrix of Metaverse, as well. Our current algorithms and the inter-operational technology furthering AI, are built on a rigid structure that is meant to deliver efficiency, maximize productivity, induce new identities to give quick answers to complex questions. Per definition, algorithms overlook the nuances in favour of simplicity. In this way, dualities that are deemed insurmountable and 'traits' such as ethnicity and gender are assumed to be – and rendered – unchangeable, as they are de-humanized, abstracted from individual biographies and emotions. Algorithms are effect-making devices, as one computer scientist told me.[7] They are meant to be highly parsimonious, elegant and slick. In the computer sciences reductionism is presented as a virtue, whereas we critical social scientists have the task to differentiate and spread issues out for more detailed examination. For us it is not worthwhile to sacrifice critical integrity for accessible causality that speeds up processes that are based on problematic data in the first place. We are aware that by narrowing down complex issues – love, passion and empathy – to a few algorithmic mnemonics, our common humanity threatens to be subtracted to zero.

Perfect imperfections

The current so-called Fourth Industrial Revolution has been fuelling the dreams of the techno-utopian community. This dreamworld has been lodged in public culture at least since H.G. Wells almost single-handedly established the science fiction genre at the beginning of the

---

[6] See for instance Stuart J. Russell and Peter Norvig, *Artificial Intelligence: A Modern Approach*, London: PEV, 2016.
[7] Interview, Oxford, United Kingdom, 10 June 2022.

twentieth century. It is not difficult to take this new strand of my analysis one step further now, and to link the idea of Superintelligence and concepts such as Metaverse to the quest for immortality, that was so central to the Enlightenment, too. Machines don't die, neither would your avatar. Today, and in particular in Silicon Valley where all the US-based tech-giants are located, techno-utopianism is already mainstream, as indicated. Its ideological adherents fund special organizations such as the Coalition for Radical Life Extension, whilst scientists working under the auspices of profit-seeking entrepreneurs are working on a range of projects, from attempting to stop cell ageing, to the practice of injecting young blood into elderly individuals. This is referred to as the 'immortality economy' and it is a market that is booming.

It was the genius critical theorists of the German Frankfurt School, Theodore Adorno and Max Horkheimer, who presented one of the most devastating critiques of the search for perfection in the 1960s, certainly in Germany and the United States. They connected it to such destructive ideas as the Aryan myth and the ideological precursor to the Holocaust, as discussed. According to them, 'calculating, instrumental, formal rationality led to the horrors of twentieth-century barbarism' including the horrors of the holocaust.[8] In this way, 'myth turns into enlightenment, and nature into mere objectivity.' Our alienation from our environment surrounding us has a heavy price, as we are increasingly detached from the real, physical world, cooped up in our mental and virtual bunker. 'The man of science knows things in so far as he can make them.'[9]

Zuckerberg, then, as a man of digital 'science' creates an alienating world – the matrix that detaches us from our habitat, the physical environment that is devalued as equal to the digital ethers of his Metaverse or the increasingly immersive messenger options on Facebook and WhatsApp. In fact, in a radically digitized world, where

[8]   Martin Jay, *The Dialectical Imagination: A History of the Frankfurt School and the Institute of Social Research 1923–1950*, London: Heinemann, 1973, p. 265.
[9]   Theodor W. Adorno and Max Horkheimer, *Dialectic of Enlightenment*, John Cumming (trans.), London: Verso, 1997, p. 9.

we would primarily interact virtually, where our emotions, even sexuality is reduced to VR projections carried by our avatars, our physical environment threatens to become entirely 'other' to us, as the balance is already favouring the Matrix. This is the crux of the meaning of alienation. Zuckerberg buys into the enlightenment hocus pocus that a perfect world can be created beyond the immanence of humanity in nature. In fact, environmental scientists have established, that some of our destructive attitudes towards the environment are exactly connected to this hubristic idea that (wo)man can afford to be alienated from nature or the physical world. Who needs the environment, if we are all attuned to living our lives in the Matrix?

Alienation and othering in favour of the perfect utopia of another world which appears cleansed, sterilized and where our avatars subtract our imperfect individualities – this is the ideology that contemporary techno-utopianism adheres to. In this world-view sameness is a virtue. It is totalitarian in this sense. Don't forget that in Aldous Huxley's famous novel *Brave New World* we encounter exactly that sterile life of seemingly perfect bliss. People get what they want, because they never want what they can't get. The digital world follows a similar logic. What you see is what you get. Avatars induce sameness, as they are abstractions and they are similar in the way that our biographies and individual emotions are not. They are certainly less complex than human beings and that's what makes them so attractive. As in *Brave New World*, avatars don't need wives, parents, or children as they are exactly unreal, detached from nature, reproductive organs or any type of living organism that is a part of our real world. Like Huxley's Hypnopaedia, VR has the effect of a vaccine administered by a totalizing system that is targeting human fallibility as a means to contain our feral sentiments. Like the Matrix, it is also a form of social control, a bit like an odourless and invisible gas infused with Diazepam, a potent mixture that numbs our human(e) senses, which are by nature-coded to be beautifully imperfect.

To sum this section up and ease us into the next: The Enlightenment was a period of immense optimism much in the same way as the techno-utopian milieu is riddled with seemingly unending possibilities, even harbouring the promise of immortality. Why should it not be possible to create a new Superintelligent AI system that is perfect, god-like, beyond human? If the Enlightenment delivered the 'Aryan man' to the pinnacle of racial selection, why should natural perfection stop there? Indeed, why might there not be a transcendental AI Machine, a Nietzschean *Übermensch* representing the perfect non-biological prototype that would rescue mankind? These are some of the methodological ideas that continue to drive the research agenda of some influential quarters of the AI lobby, without much oversight, ethical considerations or a good dose of suspicion. In this way algorithms are defeating the purpose of real productivity within society, which can only be achieved if they are based on inclusive, pluralistic and unbiased data, rather than polluted by the racist archives constituting our recent history. We want a better society, so let's work on algorithms that are representative to that end, which requires us to reveal clearly where our data problems come from in the first place.

God is white

It would be too simplistic to link the triumph of Darwinism to Nietzsche's idea of the *Übermensch*, which was subsequently perverted by the Nazis and turned into the theory of the Aryan *Herrenrasse* or master race destined to rule over humankind. In *Ecce Homo* and *On the Genealogy of Morals*, the latter written one and a half years before his mental breakdown in January 1889, Nietzsche himself qualified his concept of the *Übermensch* detaching it from Darwinism and locating the 'noble race' in the Italian Renaissance.[10] Darwin, on the other side, did locate man on the pinnacle of the organic scale pondering natural selection, which 'acts solely by the preservation of profitable

---

[10]   See further, Rüdiger Safranski, *Nietzsche: A Philosophical Biography*, London: Granta, 2003.

modifications', which is why 'extinction and natural selection' will always 'go hand in hand'.[11] But he also emphasized that he uses the term, 'Struggle for Existence', 'in a large and metaphorical sense, including dependence of one being on another'.[12] So his unwavering trust in theoretical constructions did not tempt him to overlook the inherent interdependency of the natural world and man's inevitable position within it. In fact, in his autobiography he turns his own theory into a critique of arrogance in the pursuit of scientific knowledge: 'Can the mind of man, which has, as I fully believe, been developed from a mind as low as that possessed by the lowest animal, be trusted when it draws such grand conclusions?'[13]

Despite Darwin's apparent scepticism, the idea that nature continuously progresses into something better, lends itself to the type of racial theorizing that was characteristic for the colonial 'desiring machine'. This is yet another critical theme in post-colonial studies that I would like to connect to the kind of techno-utopianism explained above. According to Robert Young, for instance, it is sexual desire 'constituted by a dialectic of attraction and repulsion' that carries along 'the threat of the fecund fertility of the colonial desiring machine, whereby a culture in its colonial operation becomes hybridized, alienated and potentially threatening to its European original through the production of polymorphously perverse people'.[14]

From this proposition, Young moves on to charter the many racial typologies of the colonized peoples that were produced in the latter part of the nineteenth century, for instance with regard to the inhabitants of Latin America, themselves heirs of some of the most sophisticated ancient civilizations of the world (yet untrained in methods of mass murder that were perfected in Europe). Young shows how children with

---

[11] Charles Darwin, *The Origin of Species*, Ware: Wordsworth, 1998, p. 133.

[12] Ibid., p. 50.

[13] Charles Darwin, 'The Descent of Man, and Selection in Relation to Sex', part 2, Paul H. Barrett and R. B. Freeman (eds), *The Works of Charles Darwin*, vol. 22, New York: New York University Press, 1989, p. 644.

[14] Robert J.C. Young, 'Colonialism and the Desiring Machine', in Gregory Castle (ed.), *Postcolonial Discourses: An Anthology*, Oxford: Blackwell, 2001, p. 87.

white fathers and negro mothers were classified as mulattos, a white father and an Indian mother produced 'mestizas' and a white father and mestiza mother, a 'creole' who could be identified by her pale-brownish complexion. Unsurprisingly, the list ends with the 'zambo-negro', the 'perfectly black' child of a black father and zamba mother.[15] Such pseudo-scientific classification was not confined to the Americas, of course. Such racism was used in India, West Asia, the African continent and within North American and European societies, too – in the West as a technique to buttress 'white' suzerainty within society, by a discourse sold as 'science'.

Adorno and Horkheimer, followed by the Italian philosopher Giorgio Agamben today, argue that it was due to the 'murder' of God that the Enlightenment erred into nihilism. According to them, this period had to entail an element of scientific arrogance and hubris, certainly towards the 'other'. Whereas before, difference was accentuated through religion, the Enlightenment codified the binaries in theories that were presented as objective laws of nature. Hence, during the Enlightenment producing alterity was professionalized. A whole array of disciplines, chief amongst them anthropology, biology and later on the social sciences, were busy turning the 'otherness' of the non-European people into an 'objective reality' that could be scientifically measured. Books such as Robert Brown's *The Races of Mankind* (1873), Comte de Gobineau's voluminous *An Essay on the Inequality of Human Races* (1853–1855), Robert Knox's *The Races of Men* (1850), Carl Linnaeus's *Systema Naturae* (1735), Frederick Marryat's *Peter Simple* (1834), Josiah Nott and George Gliddon's *Types of Mankind* (1854), Edward B. Tylor's, *Anthropology: An Introduction to the Study of Man and Civilisation* (1881) or Johann von Tschudi's *Travels in Peru* (1847), created the archives of racial politics out of which modern political systems such as Apartheid in South Africa emerged.

The social and cultural legacies of Enlightenment racism continue to haunt us and they are polluting the data sets of our techno-societies.

---

[15]   Ibid., pp. 88 ff.

Examples abound in contemporary Europe: Until today, France struggles with racism and it seems that advanced technologies don't mitigate a deeply anchored cultural aversion towards 'immigrants'. For example, despite of the integration of body-cams into the police force, i.e. small individual mobile cameras mounted on the uniforms of the French police in order to record their actions, the 'baseless' ethnic profiling of Arab and black youths as young as 10 years old continues to be flagged as human rights abuses by prominent organizations.[16] The reasons are historical, too. The most exalted French thinkers of the nineteenth century were also buying into the idiocy of racism. For example, in his *Essai sur l'inégalité des races humaines* published in 1853, the famed Count Arthur de Gobineau defined 'Semites' as a white hybrid race bastardized by a mixture with 'Blacks'. The legendary Palestinian polymath Edward Said showed, that Ernest Renan in his *Histoire Générale et Système comparé des Langues* introduced a comparable classification, opposing 'Semites' to 'Aryans'. Renan was particularly sceptical about the 'racial power' of Muslims.[17]

The current Director of the Max Planck Institute for the Study of Religious and Ethnic Diversity in Göttingen, Peter Van der Veer, has added additional material explaining how during the Enlightenment 'craniometry', the measuring of skulls and 'phrenology', a scientific method that links the size of the skull to individual's mental faculties, became the empirical focus of race science.[18] In England, race theorists even came up with biological explanations of foreign policy that 'explained' scientifically that the 'English Overman' was destined to rule the world due to his racial superiority.[19] In more recent scholarship, my perceptive colleague at Sheffield University, John Hobson, has added

---

16 Bénédicte Jeannerod, 'Body Cameras Alone Won't Stop Discriminatory Policing in France', *Human Rights Watch*, 17 July 2020. Available at <https://www.hrw.org/news/2020/07/17/body-cameras-alone-wont-stop-discriminatory-policing-france>.

17 Edward Said, *Orientalism*, London: Penguin, especially pp. 133 ff.

18 Peter Van der Veer, *Imperial Encounters: Religion and Modernity in India and Britain*, Princeton, NJ: Princeton University Press, 2001, 145–146.

19 See further Hannah Arendt, *The Origins of Totalitarianism*, 2nd edn, Cleveland, OH: World Publishing Co., 1958, p. 180.

further truth to the matter. 'For the first time in world history', Hobson comments on the Enlightenment period, 'the development of societies was assumed to be founded on permanent racial characteristics ... Special emphasis was placed – again for the first time in world history – on the importance of skin colour and genetic properties'. This section speaks to my repeated emphasis on scientific racism being a novel, and uniquely European invention. 'This was now conceived of as a permanent hierarchy and for some, though not all, scientific racists justified the subjugation of the Other (the Yellow and Black races) by the self (the Europeans).'[20]

Black is beautiful

Racism is a powerful residue of European, US and to a lesser extent Japanese modernity. We should not be surprised, therefore, that an algorithm by a software company called COMPAS caused several mistakes based on a racially charged calculus in the process of being used to predict the particular tendency of a convicted criminal to reoffend, as I mentioned also in the introduction. The algorithm devastated the lives of those at the receiving end of this racially charged calculus. When it was wrong in its predicting, it was revealed that the results were displayed differently for black and white offenders, as black offenders were flagged as particularly unworthy of probation. For instance, an African-American offender by the name of Robert Cannon was given a medium risk (6) ranking having one petty theft and no subsequent offence on his profile. A white offender by the name of James Rivelly was categorized as low risk (3), with prior offences such as domestic violence, aggravated assault, grand theft, petty theft, drug trafficking and another subsequent offence in grand theft. In another example, 'black' Brisha Borden was deemed 'high risk' (8) with four

---

[20] John Hobson, *The Eastern Origins of Western Civilisation*, Cambridge: Cambridge University Press, 2004, p. 237.

counts of juvenile misdemeanour and no subsequent offences, while 'white' Vernon Prater was considered low risk (3) with prior offences such as two armed robberies, one attempted armed robbery and one grand theft as a subsequent offence – truly staggering and shocking discrepancies here.

The data sets feeding into AI systems will be prejudiced and discriminatory, as long as modern racism is accepted as a part of our social reality, which is, of course, distinctly multicultural and mixed, now. But going back to the more specific theme of desire and racism: Scholars in Black Studies have presented dozens of outstanding books and research articles which magnify the colonial roots of the sexual fetishization of black women whose rape, it should be noted, was legalized and at times recommended as an act of racial 'purification'. Recent studies into racist AI algorithms that link black women to porn suggest that this insidious link between desire and race feeds into the data of our current systems: 'As a result of the lack of African Americans and people with deeper knowledge of the sordid history of racism and sexism working in Silicon Valley, products are designed with a lack of careful analysis about their potential impact on a diverse array of people.'[21]

Search engines are a very good reflection of this legacy which threatens to destroy all the potential benefits that inclusive algorithms under the supervision of minorities could bring about in Europe and especially in the racially charged atmosphere of the United States. Try Google on any term that is laden with forms of racism that we are all aware of: Jew, Arab, Black, Chinese, Italian, Pakistani, Irish, Turk, Hindi, Muslim, Chinese, Russian, Gay, Basque, Traveller etc., and the worse racism and bigotry is just one click away. No wonder, then, that social media sites such as Facebook and Telegram have been indicted for fomenting social unrest. We are beginning to understand why now: We have not managed to overcome the stupidities of our past.

[21] Safiya Umoja Noble, *Algorithms of Oppression: How Search Engines Reinforce Racism*, New York: New York University Press, 2018, p. 66.

History as we encounter it in our archives is a culprit, then. Many of the older generation of so-called 'great thinkers' that created much of the modern world that we inherited were anti-humanistic from our perspective today. This cultural illiteracy permeating Europe still in the nineteenth century and early-twentieth century is full of the lore of racial superiority, exactly because of the ignorance permeating those societies at that time and in many ways before. In the mainstream they displayed a lack of a stock of shared humanistic knowledge that ancient civilizations in China, Persia, Egypt, Ethiopia, Peru, Mexico and elsewhere held on to over several generations. In cultural terms and measured in accordance with truly humane ideas that are inclusive, Enlightenment Europe was surprisingly primitive and barbarian. Almost all biographies of the main engineers of European modernity are tainted by various forms of racism and sexism.

It is no accident then, that in his bestselling book about his travels through western Asia, the Tory Aristocrat, Mark Sykes (1879–1919) presented a kind of comparative 'raciology' of the peoples he encountered, their 'puzzling faces', and their indistinguishable physiognomy. Although a 'Hill Kurd can be as easily distinguished from a Bedawi as a negro from an Englishmen', Sykes established in all honesty during his travels in and around Mosul (today's Iraq), 'the intermediate races present every combination of the two types. I have seen men known as Kurds', he elaborated, 'exhibiting every Arab characteristic, and Egal-wearing village Arabs so coarse-featured as to make one doubt whether the Arabs are a handsome race. How is it that, now and then', Sykes wondered 'amid a group of roundstomached brown-skinned little rascals, tumbling in the dust of a Fellaheen village, you will see a flaxen-haired, blue-eyed child with a face that Millais would have been glad to catch a glimpse of?'[22]

Elsewhere, Sykes' puzzlement turned into disgust of these seemingly ugly people that Britain was about to rule: According to him, the

---

[22] Mark Sykes, *Dar-Ul-Islam: A Record of a Journey Through Ten of the Asiatic Provinces of Turkey*, London: Bickers & Son, 1904, 177–178.

inhabitants of Mosul were 'eloquent, cunning, excitable, and cowardly ... one of the most deplorable pictures one can see in the East diseased from years of foul living.... With minds of mudlarks and the appearance of philosophers.' Ultimately, 'they depress and disgust the observer.'[23] Such were the attitudes of the man who co-invented the map of the modern 'Middle-East', who together with his French counterpart Francois-George Picot, a comparably destructive individual, carved up the Ottoman Empire during World War I. The results of their idiotic and infamous 'lines in the sand' can be felt until today, as the arbitrary borders they promoted are the source of many conflicts besetting the region, blowing back to Europe in terms of terror campaigns and refugee waves.

The colonial gaze that seduced Sykes into that problematic racial typology and comments about the unattractiveness of some of the tribes he encountered can be connected to so called 'beauty algorithms' such as Qoves's tool, that are used for various purposes today, including facial recognition software used to police minorities as we will find out in the next chapters. At this stage it is my concern to connect today's AI world to the residues of Enlightenment legacies. So it is rather more important to point out that the beauty algorithms are distinctly racist. In 2016, for instance, the world's first international beauty contest judged solely by an algorithm crowned 44 winners. You will not be surprised that almost all of them were white as there were only a handful of women with an 'Asian' background crowned 'Miss Algorithm' and only one with a darker complexion.[24] It is almost as if Mark Sykes was on the jury.

Such racist beauty scoring is not confined to relatively innocent beauty contests. Social media platforms use it to identify 'attractive' faces in order to highlight their profiles. The trend is global now. For instance, the moderators of the most successful social media site at the

[23] Ibid., 177–178.
[24] Arwa Mahdawi, 'This AI-powered App Will Tell You if You're Beautiful – and Reinforce Biases, Too', *The Guardian*, 6 March 2021. Available at <https://www.theguardian.com/commentisfree/2021/mar/06/ai-powered-app-tell-you-beautiful-reinforce-biases>.

time of writing, TikTok, owned by the Chinese company ByteDance, were told to actively suppress videos from poor, physically challenged or seemingly 'ugly' users. *The Guardian* of London revealed in 2020 that a 'content moderation memo demanded that videos were excluded from the For You feed if they featured users with "abnormal body shape (not limited to: dwarf, acromegaly)", who are "chubby … obese or too thin" or who have "ugly facial looks or facial deformities".[25]

The South China Morning Post revealed further that social media filters, for instance on Facebook's Instagram, have had a profound impact on demands for plastic surgery. This 'selfie dysmorphia' is meant to bring the filtered image, closer to the unfiltered reality.[26] In fact, a survey by the American Academy of Facial Plastic and Reconstructive Surgery in 2017 found out that 55 per cent of surgeons revealed they had consulted patients who asked for surgery to improve the way they look in selfies – an increase from 42 per cent in 2015.[27] This trend has been compounded, too by the Covid-19 pandemic leading to a 'Zoom boom' in plastic and cosmetic surgery. We have antidotes to the idiocy of racism. We just need to inject them into our social fabric that frames the data feeding into the AI algorithms that are increasingly constituting us, in terms of our desires, looks, identities and even our sexual preferences.

SS bots

Allow me to set some additional historical signposts to contextualize my argument about the nexus between AI technology and Enlightenment racism further: Nowhere did the myth of racial

---

[25]   Alex Hern, 'TikTok "Tried to Filter out Videos from Ugly, Poor or Disabled Users"', *The Guardian*, 17 March 2020. Available at <https://www.theguardian.com/technology/2020/mar/17/tiktok-tried-to-filter-out-videos-from-ugly-poor-or-disabled-users>.

[26]   Melissa Twigg, 'How Snapchat Dysmorphia Drives Teens to Plastic Surgery to Copy Looks Phone Camera Filters Give Them', *The South China Morning Post*, 17 June 2019. Available at <https://www.scmp.com/lifestyle/fashion-beauty/article/3014543/how-snapchat-dysmorphia-drives-teens-plastic-surgery-copy>.

[27]   Ibid.

perfection do more harm than in Germany after the election of the National Socialist German Worker's Party in April 1933. The idea(l) of Aryan origins and the seemingly inevitable triumph of the German *Herrenrasse* (master race) could only be fostered within a causalistic universe that was depleted of critical thinking. Indeed, it is not too far fetched to say that Fascism is the polar opposite of a critical scientific consciousness, because Fascism educates people to take the surrounding world for granted, to submit to the leader without much questioning.

The reality of the current political set-up in some of the most highly technologized societies in the Western hemisphere, certainly the United States under Trump, has demonstrated that such critical scientific attitudes can be marginalized by crude, right-wing leaders with no real intellectual aptitude for the complexity of the world that we are living in. Social media sites compound this trend, too. An investigation by the Washington DC based NGO Tech Transparency Program revealed that 'Facebook's algorithms create an echo chamber that reinforces the views of white supremacists and helps them connect with each other.'[28] This radicalization has had a particularly devastating effect during the Covid-19 pandemic, as people spent more time online. The research conducted in 2020 and published in May of the same year established that of the 221 designated white supremacist organizations, 51 per cent (113 groups) had an active presence on approximately 153 Facebook sites. Type in 'Battle of the Nibelungen', which refers to a classic heroic epic much loved by the Nazis and re-enacted by right-wing martial arts extremists today – or any other fascist theme for that matter – and all the tech-platforms screened for this study will come up with something particularly offensive, in particular towards minorities.

In many ways the pseudo-sciences fostered by the Nazis are the extreme manifestation of the positivism that is feeding into the uncritical acceptance of algorithms and their false promise of equality and transparency that the tech-giants are accused of aiding and abetting

---

28 'White Supremacist Groups Are Thriving on Facebook', *Tech Transparency Project*, 21 May 2020. Available at <https://www.techtransparencyproject.org/articles/white-supremacist-groups-are-thriving-on-facebook>.

for the purpose of profit making. In November 2021, a Facebook 'whistle-blower' clearly set out the link between algorithms and White Supremacist and other right-wing movements: 'Facebook has realized that if they change the algorithm to be safer, people will spend less time on the site, they'll click on less ads, they'll make less money'.[29] In fact, provoked by the outrage about the storming and occupation of the Capitol in Washington DC, the former chief executive of Twitter, Jack Dorsey, admitted that the social networking site was used to organize the attacks. 'Yes,' he said according to the *New York Times*. 'But you also have to take into consideration the broader ecosystem. It's not just about the technological systems that we use.'[30]

Mark Zuckerberg made a comparable admission, when in April 2018, he testified to a US Congressional investigation into data privacy and Russian disinformation on Facebook. 'It's clear now that we didn't do enough to prevent these tools from being used for harm', Zuckerberg said. 'That goes for fake news, foreign interference in elections, and hate speech, as well as developers and data privacy.'[31] He even took personal responsibility for some of the failings: 'We didn't take a broad enough view of our responsibility, and that was a big mistake. And it was my mistake. And I'm sorry. I started Facebook, I run it, and I'm responsible for what happens here.'[32] At the same time, however, he repeatedly invoked the promise of Artificial Intelligence to improve the moderation of the platform and to filter out hate speech, obviously aware that algorithms muddle culpability. 'I am optimistic that, over a 5 to 10-year period, we will have A.I. tools that can get into some of the nuances – the

[29]   Aaron Mak, 'Frances Haugen Might Be Facebook's Biggest Threat in Years', *Slate*, 3 October 2021. Available at <https://slate.com/technology/2021/10/frances-haugen-facebook-60-minutes-whistleblower.html>.

[30]   Kate Conger, 'Jack Dorsey Says Twitter played a Role in U.S. Capitol Riot', *The New York Times*, 25 March 2021. Available at <https://www.nytimes.com/2021/03/25/business/jack-dorsey-twitter-capitol-riot.html>.

[31]   Chloe Watson, 'The Key Moments from Mark Zuckerberg's Testimony to Congress', *The Guardian*, 11 April 2018. Available at <https://www.theguardian.com/technology/2018/apr/11/mark-zuckerbergs-testimony-to-congress-the-key-moments>.

[32]   'Transcript of Mark Zuckerberg's Senate Hearing', *The Washington Post*, 10 April 2018. Available at <https://www.washingtonpost.com/news/the-switch/wp/2018/04/10/transcript-of-mark-zuckerbergs-senate-hearing/>.

linguistic nuances of different types of content to be more accurate in flagging things for our systems.' Zuckerberg admitted that 'today, we're just not there on that. So a lot of this is still reactive. People flag it to us. ...We have policies to try to make it as not subjective as possible. But, until we get it more automated, there is a higher error rate than I'm happy with.'[33]

Until today, Facebook has not fully disclosed what it knows about how its social media platforms furthered the cause of extremist groups such as QAnon that promoted the storming of the Capitol in 2021. Thereby it is not fully implementing its own Oversight Board's recommendation that it should be more transparent especially with regard to 'risks of harm posed by political leaders and other influential figures.'[34] In the end, The Oversight Board upheld Facebook's decision to suspend Donald Trump's access to post content on Facebook and Instagram, in January 2021, almost at the same time as Twitter banned Trump from his account. In an official statement, Facebook invoked AI, once again, as a means to improve their ability to flag and filter hate speech in the future, just as they did in 2018.[35]

[33] Ibid.
[34] 'The Oversight Board Upholds Former President Trump's Suspension and Finds that Facebook Failed to Impose Proper Penalty'. *The Oversight Board*, May 2021. Available at <https://oversightboard.com/news/226612455899839-oversight-board-upholds-former-president-trump-s-suspension-finds-facebook-failed-to-impose-proper-penalty/>.
[35] Guy Rosen and Monika Bickert, 'Our Response to the Violence in Washington', *Meta*, 6 January 2021. Available at <https://about.fb.com/news/2021/01/responding-to-the-violence-in-washington-dc/>.

3

Capital Punishment

Aldous Huxley can be positioned within a long tradition of anti-totalitarian thought in Britain. Like most of the British luminaries of the time, including the contrarian Eric Arthur Blair (George Orwell), Huxley hailed from a prominent family. In his *Brave New World* written in 1931, at a time when Fascist parties popped up everywhere in Europe and Soviet Communism loomed large from the East, Huxley tackled – perhaps even unconsciously – one of the main legacies of the Enlightenment at the heart of totalitarian ideologies: The search for a perfect order – utopia. This is the 'Brave New World' where sameness is celebrated, either as a form of racial purity, or a proletarian mass that overrides our individuality in favour of some skewed notion of sameness, in both cases administered by the state, which emerges as the locus for everything that is perfect. 'The price of freedom is eternal vigilance', Huxley warned in light of such threats, in an iconic interview with Mike Wallace in 1958.[1]

But even a perceptive mind such as Huxley's couldn't entirely escape the escapades of the Enlightenment a century earlier. *Brave New World* was written in 1931 and published one year later, at a time when Fascism and the Eugenics movement in Britain adopted some of the racist syntax inherited from Enlightenment thought. In an article from 1927 written for *Vanity Fair*, Huxley mirrored some of the problematic themes that made his brother Julian join the 'The British Eugenics Society movement'. According to Aldous Huxley: 'Physically and mentally defective individuals are now preserved in greater quantities

---

[1] 'Aldous Huxley Interviewed by Mike Wallace (1958). Available at <https://www.youtube.com/watch?v=alasBxZsb40>.

than at any other period'. Echoing some of the extremist social Darwinist views that were common since the Enlightenment, he warned that 'Humanitarianism has provided the incentive, political security and medical science the means, for achieving this preservation of those whom nature would regard as unfit to survive.' It is not only that these humans are considered unfit genetically. According to Huxley, there is an economic trade-off as the 'average ability of the unskilled worker is lower than the average ability of the skilled and professional worker ... given differences in the rate of multiplication, the inferior types are being increased at the expense of the superior types'.[2]

The idea that human perfection can – and needs – to be engineered by a superior class of people did not start, nor end with Hitler, then. Like many other 'liberals' of his generation, Huxley was seduced by a fake science. He was certainly no Fascist. But until today 'liberals' do toy with utopian ideas about human perfection. The Nazis are rightly indicted by scholars as the main culprit for this systematic dehumanization, as being human always also means being imperfect. On the one side, the obsession of the Nazis with racial purity was a perverted extension of the entanglement of the Enlightenment with natural selection and the inevitable superiority of the 'white' race. On the other side, it also gives us an insight into how a world of separated communities would look like, as the mass murder of the Jews, homosexuals, Gypsies and the physically and mentally impaired, was also an effort to create a form of biopolitical purity. Hence, this was a strategy to be independent from the undue influence of any 'others' in terms of race *and* space. This rather important biopolitics of exclusion has been largely overlooked by post-colonial theorists, even by the founder of this sub-discipline, the late Edward Said himself.

The Nazis did not only find it impossible to recognize the *Herrenrasse*, without freezing the 'other' into an unchanging object, without attributing to the Jews a set of racial characteristics that made them

---

2   Aldous Huxley, 'A note on Eugenics', *Vanity Fair*, October 1927. Available at <https://archive.vanityfair.com/article/1927/10/a-note-on-eugenics>.

different from the 'truly' German nation. They attempted to thoroughly detach themselves from the impact of all existence that they deemed 'unworthy'. They tried to present to us a space that was totally cleansed – the perfectly 'white' utopia. Only in the ability of fascist ideology to deliver perfection, with no critical acumen or intellectual enquiry, could they believe in the 'manifest destiny' personified by the *Führer*. 'The Fascists do not view the Jews as a minority', write Adorno and Horkheimer, 'but as an opposing race, the embodiment of the negative principle'.[3] In other words, the mass murder of the Jews, homosexuals, the Sinti and Roma and the mentally and physically impaired, were efforts to create a true and absolute genealogy; a historical tale dotted with heroic Aryan figures and racially pure personalities that would deliver the world from its seemingly imperfect existence.

The central policies of the Nazis are reflections of this effort to create purity, to cleanse the self from *any* impingement by the alien 'races'. It started out with exclusionary laws: the Law on the Overcrowding of German Schools, the Law on the Reconstitution of the German Civil Service, and it evolved into the geopolitics of ghettoization and the concentration camps, which were meant to realize the territorial/spatial contraction of the 'other', thus maximizing distance to him/her. At the same time, the total state and total war functioned in order to enhance the coherence of the Aryan self. The *Endlösung*, the effort to obliterate all Jews, was a culmination of these two processes: It symbolized the last-ditch effort to reverse and totally negate the interdependence between the Aryan *Herrenrasse* and its Jewish 'other' *par excellence*.

With Nazism, the totalitarian methodologies I have examined above and their causalistic fallacies come full circle. The total state, total war, the total obliteration of the Jews (or *Endlösung*), all of these manifestations of 'National Socialism' could only derive from an uncompromising belief in an absolute historical teleology that had distilled the Aryan nation and its destiny to rule the world in a grand

---

[3]   Theodor W. Adorno and Max Horkheimer, *Dialectic of Enlightenment*, John Cumming (trans.), London: Verso, 1997, p. 168.

spectacle of natural selection. In other words, the Nazis perceived themselves to be both the effect of history and the enforcer to bring about the end of all racial struggles, to create a new Over-Mensch. Ultimately, the 'Third Reich' was not considered to be a random event. It was seen and portrayed as an inevitable effect of humanity's progress that made manifest the successive forms of a primordial historical intention. The 'Third Reich' was perceived to usher in a better future for humanity: the end of all racial clashes. Therefore, the Nazis called their project the Reich that will last for a thousand years – das Tausendjährige Reich.

So within the cosmos of the European Enlightenment everything was considered possible, and the Nazis felt that they could make everything happen in that exact tradition. So they rushed from conquest to conquest without a period of strategic consolidation. Now that History had delivered Germany's mission and now that the natural world had distilled the Aryan race, the total state must hasten to accomplish the destiny that has been bestowed upon it: the all encompassing liberation of mankind and the genetic engineering of a new superior Mensch. This straight *Autobahn* could only be taken because it was cemented by ideological fallacies due to the absence of criticism, which was purged from society as intellectuals, poets, artists and contrarian professors were declared 'degenerates' by the Nazis. In this way, the Führer was the truth, as there was no one left to contradict. *Der Führer hat immer recht*, the Leader is always right, said Rudolf Hess; *In tal senso il fascismo è totalitario*, in this sense, fascism is totalitarian, Mussolini maintained. And so the infallible total state swallowed the individual in order to make true its promise. This destruction of individuality is the essence of totalitarianisms of any kind.

Sociacide

We can establish a fundamental signpost at this stage of our discussion: Totalitarianism is not only about politics. There is a social element to it, there is this emphasis on homogeneity, and race plays a crucial role in any type of totalitarian thought and strategy. Therefore, racism is not merely about your ethnicity or skin colour. In fact, racism serves two crucial ordering principles of contemporary societies pretty much all over the world, including here, in the so-called 'West': First, racism is a social strategy of dividing and ghettoizing communities within the population into a hierarchy of good and bad, functional and dysfunctional, rich and poor. It is in this way that society can be governed and managed. Second, racism is not only an ordering device to make society more governable. It reveals itself as a social war that kills without direct confrontation, without a declaration of war. There are no armies and no bombs in this battle. Murder is disguised, it could be the end of your career or it could be your social, ethnic and other form of exclusion. Foucault was right on this one, even if he died before experiencing the totalizing effect of technology that we are focusing on: 'In a normalising society, race or racism is the precondition that makes killing acceptable.'[4] Killing, in this case, does not merely refer to physical death, but includes our social murder, our 'sociacide'.

Such sociacidal mechanisms are deeply embedded in AI technology. Comprehensive research into algorithms used by US police departments for the purpose of 'predictive policing' have demonstrated that the machine-learning models are based on racially biased data.[5] According to figures released by the US Department of Justice, black individuals are more than twice as likely to be arrested, than if you are white. Moreover, it is five times more likely that a black person is stopped without a just cause than a white individual.[6]

4   Michel Foucault, *Society Must be Defended: Lectures at the Collège de France*, Mauro Bertani and Alessandro Fontana (eds), David Macey (trans.), London: Penguin, 2004, 256.
5   See Will Douglas Heaven, 'Predictive Policing Algorithms Are Racist. They Need to Be Dismantled', *MIT Technology Review*, 17 July 2020. Available at <https://www.technologyreview.com/2020/07/17/1005396/predictive-policing-algorithms-racist-dismantled-machine-learning-bias-criminal-justice/>.
6   'Statistical Briefing Book', *US Department of Justice, Office of Juvenile Justice and Delinquency Prevention*. Available at <https://www.ojjdp.gov/ojstatbb/crime/ucr.asp?table_in=2>.

The American Civil Liberties Union found that face recognition software such as Amazon's Rekognition are equally racially biased, as 28 members of the US Congress, mostly people of colour, were incorrectly matched with mugshot images of criminal offenders. In Britain, dozens of black Uber drivers, have been repeatedly prevented from working due to what they say is 'racist' facial verification technology. Uber uses Microsoft Face API software on its app to verify the identity of their drivers. The algorithm underlying the software has difficulty properly recognizing individuals with darker skin tones. Companies such as Microsoft and Amazon aggressively market their Face Recognition technology to law enforcement agencies in particular in the United States, and there is increasing demand for such technology all over the world.

Exclusion, ghettoization, discrimination and other forms of racially charged policies, continue to enforce the self–other geopolitics that Enlightenment racism was meant to engineer with deadly force all over the world, as the social exclusion of 'others', in particular ethnic minorities and women, is embedded in our current algorithms. Racism has been a part of the DNA of our social systems at least since the onset of Western modernity. Algorithmic bias embedded in any computational system governing our institutions threatens to encode this racism and to make it untraceable, normalized and therefore permanently opaque. Furthermore, it has been my contention that racism amounts to an economic war that is played out within societies. Several studies have already established that in the United States mortgages are more expensive or altogether unavailable for minority groups; students get screened out of top schools and at some universities black students were up to four times more likely to be considered 'high risk' compared to white students.[7]

The medical field is affected, too. In the healthcare services, black patients are more likely to be denied life-saving care, at the same time as

---

[7]   See further Jon Kleinberg, Jens Ludwig, Sendhil Mullainathan, Cass R. Sunstein, 'Discrimination in the Age of Algorithms', *Journal of Legal Analysis*, 10 (2018), 113–174.

white patients with the same level of illness are more likely to receive treatment. In the United States, data used by health care providers overwhelmingly discriminate against darker skinned people. For instance, AI-driven technology used by dermatologists in order to detect skin cancer are missing samples of darker skin types.[8] According to research by the American Academy of Dermatology that I perused for this study, fair-skinned people are at the highest risk for contracting skin cancer. However, the mortality rate for African Americans is considerably higher: Their five-year survival rate is 73 per cent, compared with 90 per cent for white Americans.[9] The human skin as a topographical object of racism continues to decide about life and death. In terms of policing, too, black individuals are targeted more frequently by predictive algorithms for drug use, despite the pattern of drug abuse being comparable across the different communities.[10] There is no conspiracy by some kind of sinister Nazi headquarter to discriminate and exclude minorities as was the case in the past. It is simply that our algorithms mimic some of the legacies of that tainted Enlightenment history of Europe and North America, in particular. We continue to understand why, now.

Capitalism and death

I have argued that the Enlightenment was born in hubris, in the myth of the purity of race, and that it is out of this constellation that the idea of 'modern man' emerged. This particularly violent subject of history almost obliterated 'the other', not only quite literally in the many

---

8   Angela Lashbrook, 'AI-Driven Dermatology Could Leave Dark-Skinned Patients Behind', *The Atlantic*, 16 August 2018. Available at <https://www.theatlantic.com/health/archive/2018/08/machine-learning-dermatology-skin-color/567619/>.

9   See 'Skin Cancer in People of Color', *American Academy of Dermatology Association*, no date. Available at <https://www.aad.org/public/diseases/skin-cancer/types/common/melanoma/skin-color>.

10 See 'Report: Algorithms Are Worsening Racism, Bias, Discrimination', *Public Citizen*, 17 August 2021. Available at <https://www.citizen.org/news/report-algorithms-are-worsening-racism-bias-discrimination/>.

massacres colonialism and fascism engendered, but also epistemologically. The notion of development – whether *Hegelian*, characterized as a law of conscious intellectual maturing, *Darwinian*, manifesting itself in the perfection of biological change, or *Comtian*, promising ethical improvement through the control over the material and psychological environment – was meant to minimize the West's reciprocal relation to the rest of humanity. The Enlightenment didn't hail the victory of humanism – it gave impetus to a vicious trend of de-humanization that continues until today.

So far we have established that there existed a continuous effort, in Europe and North America, to leave the 'other' behind, not only in terms of race, but also in terms of space. Racism has both a spatial dynamic, for instance the politics of exclusion, and a biological one, for example the politics of genetic purification. This is how the hiatus of the Enlightenment, apart from life-affirming innovations, also detached the idea of the West from the rest of humanity. Belief in origins that are not interdependent, in a human race that is by necessity hierarchized, the futile effort to invent a 'liberalized' syntax that is devoid of reciprocity, are characteristic of this self-inflicted loneliness of the 'European white man'. Because of its immense velocity, the repercussion of this violence of the Enlightenment is an essential component of our contemporary AI-ruled social and political reality.

We have to dig even deeper, now, in order to have a full understanding about some of the root causes of contemporary forms of racism, sexism and other anti-human strategies. In an important contribution published in 2019, Shoshana Zuboff set out how the so-called 'tech-giants' – in particular Amazon, Google and Facebook – have created a form of 'surveillance capitalism' that is exploitative and demeaning.[11] In a crucial section of her book she describes the typically messianic language of tech-utopianists such as the founder of Facebook, Mark Zuckerberg, that we have already touched upon in the last chapter.

---

[11] Shoshana Zuboff, *The Age of Surveillance Capitalism: The Fight for a Human Future at the New Frontier of Power*, London: Public Affairs, 2019.

Speaking in 2017 at Facebook's developers' conference, Zuckerberg used terms such as 'moral validation', and giving people 'purpose and hope', by connecting them into a 'global community', which he identified as a civilizational task. Human beings would enter this new phase of social evolution under the aegis of Facebook or Meta as the company is called today. As Zuboff rightly interjects: The 'surveillance capitalists fail to mention that the magical age they envision comes at a price' as their enterprise expands 'toward totality ... and overwhelms every source of friction in the service of its economic imperative ... all power yearns toward totality.'[12]

Zuboff dismantles an important effect of technology without rooting 'surveillance capitalism' systematically in the totalitarian effects that the *zeitgeist* of the Enlightenment provoked. It was not a coincidence that the systematic detachment of the West from the rest of humanity occurred parallel to the discovery of money as an instrument to satisfy desires, imaginations, dreams. The West inscribed a metaphysical meaning to the material world in the way that no other culture did in the history of humanity. In the Middle Ages, money was not associated with making dreams come true, in the same way as it was envisaged by Enlightenment thinkers to bring about ultimate satisfaction in the here and now, rather than in paradise, as Christianity postulated. In this way the European Enlightenment enchanted the material world heaving it to a 'godly' status. Economics, enterprise, business, not merely to safeguard a decent living standard, but as a means to attain ultimate happiness. The lonely 'white man' created this golden calf during a period when he tried to rob himself of the interdependence he used to have with the rest of the world; when he became disenchanted as Max Weber said, when he murdered God as Friedrich Nietzsche alluded to, when the body was turned into a machine and commodity measured by its usefulness as Descartes accomplished in his seminal 'A Discourse on Method'.

---

[12] Ibid., 403–404.

We have been told, more systematically since the eighteenth and nineteenth centuries, that money has maximal causalistic efficacy, that it is a substitute for most things, that it makes things happen. 'Every man is rich or poor', the godfather of capitalism, the Scottish thinker Adam Smith wrote at the time. He is rich or poor 'according to the degree in which he can afford to enjoy the necessaries, conveniences, and amusements of human life'.[13] Suddenly, money was not merely about survival anymore. Money was also about desire and being happy. On a more basic level and comparable to words and emotions, Adam Smith says that money designates meaning to our surrounding world; today for instance the price of an *haute couture* brand such as Christian Dior, Prada or Chanel determines its value for us. Money also allocates our place in society, e.g. whether we are rich or poor. As such, capital has an ordering effect, much in the same way as we established in our discussion about racism.

Furthermore, as long as we have enough of it, Smith seems to say, money makes us believe that we can create reality. Capitalism promises to integrate us into a better world in exactly this way, as the wretched of the earth, the poor, dwell in their favelas outside of the glitzy neighbourhoods of the rich. Money buys commodities, prestige, pleasure and happiness. The capitalist has habituated us to accept that money makes the world turn round. This integrative effect of money is a core incentive of the tech-utopianists today, as well – just that the material world has been extended into the virtual realm, one of the great economies of scale that capitalism has conquered with incredible speed. As Mark Zuckerberg said in 2019 with reference to what I called the Matrix in the previous chapter: 'If you think about it from the business perspective, enabling creators to be able to create this massively larger digital economy of goods and people to use them in a lot of different ways, I think that all makes sense.'[14]

---

[13] Adam Smith, *The Wealth of Nations*, Vol. 1, London: Dent, 1910, p. 26.
[14] 'An Interview with Mark Zuckerberg' about the Metaverse', *Stratechery*, 28 October 2021. Available at <https://stratechery.com/2021/an-interview-with-mark-zuckerberg-about-the-metaverse/>.

The essential turn that we are being embroiled in here, is the expansion of capitalism from our real material reality into the virtual world. In the process of this metamorphosis we are compelled to consume everywhere, spurned on by our 'Alexas' in the bedroom, the 'Siris' on our I-phones, and the AI-powered advertisement flooding our computers. Those who can, indulge in the bliss of this market, those who can't are left behind and ghettoized, because they don't consume. In this way, AI technology buttresses and furthers the stratification of society into 'classes' and categories such as old and young, 'hip' and undesirable, rich and poor.

Deadly transactions

At the heart of the capitalist system, there lies another factor that is crucial to our AI-powered algorithmic world and that is the process of transaction. Transaction, quite literally, denotes the immediate transition from one action into another. A transaction 'grabs' reality, immediately turning it into something else. When you go out to buy a new pair of sunglasses you are already influenced by the image you seek to adopt, because your private communication with your technological devices is determined by advertisement and marketing. The same applies to any other item you buy through a transaction, as they all come with pre-configured psychological marketing effects. Even food is marketed, for instance for being healthy. The point I am trying to make is not that all of our tastes are steered by a grand capitalist conspiracy. But that we are continuously propelled to consume, whether we like it or not, which explains the constant intervention into our lives.[15] There is, then, in our digitized reality no escaping the pressure to consume through a transaction. In fact, algorithms are deemed particularly useful in the business world, exactly because they speed up our ability

---

[15] Maša Galič, Tjerk Timan and Bert-Jaap Koops, 'Bentham, Deleuze and Beyond: An Overview of Surveillance Theories from the Panopticon to Participation', *Philosophy and Technology*, 30 (2017), 9–37.

to transact, which makes consumption much easier. Remember the world without ordering things on the internet? Most of you, probably don't. In this psycho-profiling, algorithmic online bazaar, our private realm is made public in order to increase our visibility for the sellers/ the state and any other realm of society that wants to sell us something.[16] When perceptive scholars deliberate about the 'Algorithm dispositif', it is such digital psycho-manipulation that they are referring to.[17]

But I am more interested in the psychology of transactions, here. We can include a bit of Karl Marx the philosopher, before he was seduced by totalitarian thought in his Communist Manifesto co-authored with Friedrich Engels and published in 1848. Marx puts particular emphasis on this ability of transaction as a mechanism to produce reality, to integrate us into the material world, and by doing so, gives us a (false) sense of belonging, a bit like some people talking to their Alexas as if they are their confidantes.

Marx argued that money converts our 'wishes from something in the realm of imagination, translates them from their mediated, imagined or willed existence into their *sensuous, actual* existence – from imagination to life, from imagined being into real being'.[18] For instance, buying things gives us a moment of satisfaction, even happiness, as we integrate something from the alien reality out there, into our personal space, thus making the world a tiny bit more familiar and satisfactory. It's essentially that 'buzz' that you feel when you acquire something. For a very short moment, consuming gives us what it takes from us more overwhelmingly: Serotonin. This is how you can become a shopaholic, a pathology that social psychologists call 'oniomania'. The cognitive impulse is hormonal and cognitive. Your body and mind have been coded to be satisfied by

---

[16] Zeynep Tufekci, 'Engineering the Public: Big data, Surveillance and Computational Politics', *First Monday*, 19, No. 7 (2014). Available at <https://firstmonday.org/article/view/4901/4097>.

[17] See further Davide Panagia, 'The Algorithm Dispositif (Notes towards an Investigation)', *AI Pulse Papers*. Available at <https://aipulse.org/the-algorithm-dispositif-notes-towards-an-investigation/>.

[18] Karl Marx, 'The Power of Money', in idem., *Economic and Philosophical Manuscripts of 1844*, Moscow: Foreign Languages Publishing House, 1961, p. 140, emphasis in original.

buying things. Psychologists treat the condition with serotonin infusions among other therapies, exactly because oniomania is an effect of capitalist intrusions into your mind and body. Marx was right about the potentially destructive effects of such 'false consciousness', even if he was wrong about the political remedies.

For Marx such transactions or 'mediations' show the '*truly creative power*' of money as it manages to transform the '*real essential powers of man and nature* into what are merely abstract conceits and therefore *imperfections* – into tormenting chimeras – just as it transforms *real imperfections and chimeras* – essential powers which are really impotent ... into *real powers* and *faculties*.[19] Donald Trump is, by most standards available, an imperfect, if rich politician, and would be an example for this power of money to turn real imperfections into real power. Conversely, and in a critical interpretation of the dictum of Marx, minorities would be doubly punished in any capitalist society if they are financially inept to secure their interest. They would be poor *and* discriminated against because of the colour of their skin and/or their gender/sexuality. For minorities, being poor amounts to a death sentence. Their real power and faculties would be drowned by those who can buy themselves out of their own imperfections and chimeras, exactly by the Donald Trumps of this world.

Let's dig deeper. What does it mean when in our current era someone like Donald Trump in the USA or Jair Bolsonaro in Brazil can assume an office that they are not fit for in terms of the competence that it requires? It means that the power of money in capitalist societies that are formally democratic, such as Brazil and the USA, can manufacture reality, that it has truly creative powers of the type that people in the Middle Ages exclusively associated with God and the Sovereign (the monarch). So the Enlightenment created a form of capitalism that can sustain a material world that is not dependent on nature (thus the environmental degradation of the planet that it caused), nor rationality (thus Trump and Bolsonaro's Covid-19 denial). But not only that. Today,

---

[19]   Ibid.

capitalism has not merely ravaged the natural world. Capitalism has created a virtual reality that distances the individual almost entirely from nature and society. In this process of individualization, the I-phone Mensch becomes nothing but one IP number amongst the totality of digitized consumers – a Gmail account, an avatar, a small dot-com in the infinitesimal Neural Network of the AI superhighway.

In that way, Capitalism perpetuates its own reality. In its effort to seek out more and more consumers it has to seek out new markets, economies of scale. In this sense it has to be totalitarian. This line of thought explains why it had to be the tech-giants that have aggregated more powers than any capitalist conglomerate in the history of this planet, including the East India Company, which spearheaded the British Empire. Technology is all about facilitating transactions. In fact, algorithms are nothing but embedded mnemonic transactions. Therefore, in this phase of human history, capitalism doesn't merely dominate the material world as Marx chartered, but the even more immersive virtual world, the Matrix as I called it. All founders of the main tech-companies completely adhere to this capitalist logic in word and in deed. As Bill Gates wrote in a recent review of a study on *The Future of Capitalism*:

> Ultimately, I agree with [the author] that 'capitalism needs to be managed, not defeated.' We should do more to curb its excesses and minimize its negative aspects. But no other system comes close to delivering the innovations and economic growth that capitalism has sparked around the world. This is worth remembering as we consider its future.[20]

Gates is a self-avowed capitalist, the same as Jeff Bezos, the founder of Amazon, Mark Zuckerberg, and the head of Tesla and SpaceX, Elon Musk. As capitalists they share a common ideology (and legitimately so). But whether or not this ideology is good for humanity is a very

---

[20] Bill Gates, 'Is There a Crisis in Capitalism?', *GatesNotes*, 20 May 2019. Available at <https://www.gatesnotes.com/Books/The-Future-of-Capitalism>.

different question, of course. If Herbert Marcuse, one of the doyens of the aforementioned Frankfurt School and a true visionary and humanist were still alive, he would probably join me in pointing out some of the dangers of capitalist extremism. As he rightly pointed out in the 1970s: "By virtue of the way in which it has organized its technological base, contemporary post-industrial society tends to be totalitarian." For Marcuse, totalitarianism was not merely a political phenomenon. As I have argued in this chapter, it can also be a 'non-terroristic economic technical co-ordination which operates through the manipulation of needs by vested interests ... Not only a specific form of government or party rule makes for totalitarianism, but also a specific system of production.'[21] We have established that the capitalist ideology underlying the digitized systems of production of the tech-giants displays that totalitarian claim and effect that Marcuse points to.

The not so hidden hand of digital imperialism

Marcuse rightly points out that through technology, capitalism exerts a totalitarian claim, that it usurps as much as it integrates. This is very similar to what his Iranian contemporary Jalal al-e Ahmad termed 'the machine', which according to him stifled the West as much as the rest of the world.[22] In al-e Ahmad and Marcuse, predatory capitalism stands indicted as one of the main self-harming manifestations of Western modernity. But al-e Ahmad gives us more. As one of the greatest minds of his generation, he deprecated the monstrous effects of Western modernity for its dehumanizing excesses from 1960s Tehran. The warning of al-e Ahmad was by no means restricted to Iran and the Global South. The West, too was suffering from the machine as Western capital spirals out of its firmly established spatial locus (its core) and

---

[21] Herbert Marcuse, *Towards a Critical Theory of Society*, London: Routledge, 2001, p. 50.
[22] Jalal al-e Ahmad, *Plagued by the West (Gharbzadegi)*, translated from the Persian by Paul Sprachman, New York: Caravan, 1982, p. 31.

seeks out new economies of scale in order to multiply globally and virtually, in order to override cultures and to integrate them into one whole that is centred around problematic notions about how life should be organized and what happiness entails in the first place.

Capitalists repeat time and time again that their project claims the whole world. At least from 1492 onwards, but more violently in the eighteenth and nineteenth centuries, this outward trend manifested itself in imperial domination and colonial extension, the critique of which was so central to the work of intellectuals from the Global South – Anibal Quijano al-e Ahmad, Shariati, Iqbal, Nkrumah, Fanon, to name but a few. We find evidence for their theories in the biographies of the most prominent figures of the European Enlightenment, whose statues are being dismantled as I write these lines exactly because of their inhumanity: Lord Cromer, who in 1894 declined the post of Viceroy of India and refused ten years later the position of Secretary of State for Foreign Affairs in order to become the British Consul General in Egypt, put it bluntly; 'the Englishman straining far over to hold his loved India [has to] plant a firm foot on the banks of the Nile'.[23] Thus, a highly monopolistic, core-periphery dichotomy was economically realized. '[I]n order to save the 40,000,000 inhabitants of the United Kingdom from a bloody civil war', Cecil Rhodes famously concluded, 'we colonial statesmen must acquire new lands to settle the surplus population, to provide new markets for the goods produced by them in the factories and mines. The Empire', Rhodes warned, 'is a bread and butter question. If you want to avoid civil war, you must become imperialists'.[24]

The imperial bureaucrats were convinced of the law of expansion. Indeed, they deemed it to be what Kipling famously referred to as the 'white man's burden' to govern the subject races. It is in this sense that I am treating imperialism as yet another outgrowth of the racism

---

[23] From a letter Lord Cromer wrote in 1882, quoted in Hannah Arendt, *The Origins of Totalitarianism*, 2nd edn, Cleveland, OH: World Publishing Co., 1958, p. 211.

[24] Cecil Rhodes cited in Vladimir I. Lenin, *Imperialism: The Highest Stage of Capitalism*, New York: International Publishers, 1939, p. 79.

of the Enlightenment. Buoyed by the discourse of their age and the ground-breaking discoveries of their contemporaries, the imperial bureaucrats exhibited a total belief in their cause. They were convinced that a single, global empire was necessary and possible. The digital economy is imperialistic in this expansive sense, too. It neatly connects to the exploitation of human and natural resources for capitalist gain, just that the new commodity that is mined is our personal data. With the special access that companies such as Google have to our behaviour online, the data that you give away with every click on the internet and on your mobile phone, it is now possible to have immediate access to your individual preferences, emotions, thought patterns. In this way, the digital economy satisfies one of the main principles of capitalism: The extraction imperative – from slaves, to oil to data.[25]

The most recent themes in the scholarship on this issue are indicative of my argument and link it back to the colonial period during the heydays of the European Enlightenment: data colonization, digital imperialism, etc. For instance, apart from the United States, the top 10 internet users are all located in the global south/east. India is number one with 270 million users, almost 80 million more than the USA, which is second, followed by Indonesia, Brazil, Mexico, Philippines, Vietnam, Thailand, Egypt and Turkey.[26] Yet out of Facebook's 15 data centres, 10 are in the United States, 3 in the United Kingdom, one in Finland and one in Indonesia. Facebook can extract the data from all over the world and store it in their data silos without paying us any transaction fees. The actual business model only survives with the access to this free data, as it predicts and categorizes our consumer preferences and psychology for the targeted advertisements that we are then bombarded with. The Information Technology and Innovation Foundation, a very well networked think

[25] See further Michael Kwet, 'Digital Colonialism: US Empire and the New Imperialism in the Global South', *Race and Class*, 60, No. 4 (2019), 3–26.

[26] 'Leading Countries Based on Facebook Audience Size as of January 2022', *Statista*, 8 March 2022. Available at <https://www.statista.com/statistics/268136/top-15-countries-based-on-number-of-facebook-users/>.

tank in Washington DC puts the political stakes in martial, yet analytically eye-opening terms:

> For the past quarter-millennium, each emerging wave of general-purpose technologies has widened the scope of global economic integration, raising new questions about international governance and national economic competition. The rise of the digital economy over the last two decades has further deepened and widened global integration as the Internet and related technologies have allowed firms to more easily attain global reach, while at the same time linking the world more closely in a web of information. But there is also a large countervailing force: an autocratic, non-democratic country – China – that is threatening to wrest global leadership in these technologies, with attendant social, political, economic, and security implications.[27]

Leaving aside the jibe against China for a moment, this paragraph encapsulates all the major premises that capitalists adhere to: Global expansion and total penetration for the purpose of profit and global power. A humble DC think tank absorbing all the ideological precepts of neo-liberal economics as it evolved out of Adam Smith's 'The Wealth of Nations': This is the structural, even ideological realm of thinking that I have been repeatedly alluding to in this study.

Yet today, it is not exclusively the military, nor the state that is the key social force and political locus. It is the purveyors of the algorithmic rationale that are in charge, even if their company profile doesn't include spearheading traditional wars. I mentioned Donald Trump as someone who is the synthesis of capital and power and the best example how competence can be mimicked and positions can be bought. But him being barred from Twitter and Facebook is also a good example for the overriding powers of the tech-giants whose ability to control and affect is certainly not second to that of the state – even the traditional military-industrial complex – as it is Google and Microsoft that are signing

---

[27] Robert D. Atkinson, 'A U.S. Grand Strategy for the Global Digital Economy', *Information Technology and Innovation Foundation*, 19 January 2021. Available at <https://itif.org/ publications/2021/01/19/us-grand-strategy-global-digital-economy>.

multibillion dollar contracts with the Pentagon outstripping, by far, Boeing and BAE. It is the not-so-hidden hand of technology and its current monopolists, in other words, that is creating a social, political and virtual reality that is all about expansion and therefore intensely alienating. Whoever tells you otherwise, is part of that ideological movement.

4

Techno-Imperialism

At the beginning of the 1990s, when the Soviet empire imploded, no one among the learned in the United States could get around Francis Fukuyama and his theory of an impending 'end of history'. I studied in Washington DC a few years after the end of the Cold War attending a scholarship programme in the nation's capital, whilst interning at the US Chamber of Commerce just opposite the White House. In one of the rather more distinct seminars, I remember the brave Daniel Ellsberg deliberating about the historical moment, which he compared to the euphoria in the period after the Second World War.[1] Many thinkers got caught up in the intensity of the moment and got carried away by its intoxicating promise of a 'new world order', a new 'American' century.

At the time, Fukuyama was very close to the so-called 'neo-conservative' movement in the US, that was starting to capitalize on former President Bill Clinton's sexual escapades in the White House. Their euphoria about the end of the Cold War ushered in a short period when the US thought to dominate world politics as the only remaining hegemon. For Fukuyama, there was no competition to the US model and its mixture of democracy and neo-liberal capitalism. Only a decade later, it all turned out to be a pipedream.

The end of history slipped away. Instead, the short-lived 'unipolar moment' was ended in the trenches of the so-called 'wars on terror' in Afghanistan (2002) and Iraq (2003), which eroded some of the ethical

---

[1] Ellsberg published the so-called 'Pentagon Papers', which contributed to the ending of the Vietnam war. The Pentagon Papers revealed that the US had secretly expanded its war efforts in Vietnam. The unredacted version of the documents has been posted by the National Archives in the United States. See here: <https://www.archives.gov/research/pentagon-papers>.

foundations that give sustenance to any democratic system and for which elected elites must be held accountable. The torture at Abu Ghraib, the death and destruction that the wars brought about without any strategic success, heralded the beginning of the end of the 'American century' that the neo-cons wanted to bring about with such desperate vehemence. After the terror attacks on the United States on 11 September 2001, Fukuyama wrote that 'time is on the side of modernity, and I see no lack of US will to prevail';[2] yet two decades later he conceded: 'The long-term sources of American weakness and decline are more domestic than international.'[3]

The death and destruction that the invasions of Afghanistan and Iraq brought about left an indelible stain on the idea of 'American' exceptionalism. Like a Diva that is past her prime, the US left the stage kicking and screaming. Certainly, this process was merely accelerated with the outrageous Presidency of Donald Trump and the excesses that he presided over, which almost inevitably culminated in the storming of the Capitol and the catastrophic death toll that the coronavirus brought about in the country. The end of history never really occurred. Fukuyama's theory was quickly relegated to ideological wishful thinking, rather than a serious scholarly contribution to the future of humankind.

But I have started with this idea that the West can and should end history because it is yet another train of thought that can be traced back to the European Enlightenment. Fukuyama adopted his method and indeed the phrase 'end of history' from one of the philosophical giants of the nineteenth century – the engineer of the 'West' as a concept and consciousness: The German Georg Wilhelm Friedrich Hegel (1770–1831).

In his iconic study, *The Phenomenology of Spirit* (1807), which is one of the foundational texts of German idealism, Hegel famously put

---

[2] Francis Fukuyama, 'The West Has Won', *The Guardian*, 11 October 2001. Available at <https://www.theguardian.com/world/2001/oct/11/afghanistan.terrorism30>.

[3] 'Francis Fukuyama on the End of American Hegemony', *The Economist*, 18 August 2021. Available at <https://www.economist.com/by-invitation/2021/08/18/francis-fukuyama-on-the-end-of-american-hegemony>.

forward a concept of historical development that was particularly dependent on temporal sequences. This periodization of history would act as a focal point for all major European philosophers that followed him, and on a wide spectrum, from the 'historical-materialism' of Karl Marx to the 'genealogical' lens of Friedrich Nietzsche, who in turn, influenced twentieth-century 'post-structuralist' thinkers such as Foucault, Derrida and others.

In a major intellectual tour de force, Hegel differentiated between four phases in the birth and demise of civilizations following a visibly anthropomorphic approach to the history of humankind: The period of birth and original growth, that of maturity, that of 'old age' and that of dissolution and death. Thus, for example, the history of Rome is conceived of as passing through the phase from its foundation down to the Second Punic War in the first phase; from the second Punic War to the consolidation of the Principate by Caesar in the second phase; from this consolidation to the triumph of Christianity in the third phase; and from the third century AD to the fall of Byzantium in the last phase. Similarly, Hegel argued that ancient Oriental history can be divided into four 'sub-phases', which corresponded to four political orders: the 'theocratic-despotism' of ancient China, the 'theocratic-aristocracy' of India, the 'theocratic-monarchy' of Persia, and finally the dichotomization of spirit and matter attributed to the civilization of ancient Egypt.

From the perspective of Hegel, 'the Orient', failed in its mission to solve the 'riddle of man' for humankind. The solution to it, and to history as a whole, was to be found in the 'West', a powerful idea and concept that never existed before the Enlightenment and that Hegel helped to create. Presumably, that is why according to the Oedipus myth, the Sphinx travelled to Greece and why the Owl of Minerva spread its wings in the Orient, only to settle finally in the Occident. According to these metaphors, analogies and Hegel's methodology, the 'West' was particularly dependent on the German spirit (*Geist*):

> History of the World travels from East to West, for Europe is absolutely *the end of history*, Asia the beginning. The History of the World has an East ... Here rises the outward physical Sun, and in the West it sinks

down: here consentaneously rises the Sun of self-consciousness, which *diffuses a nobler brilliance*. The History of the World is the discipline of the uncontrolled natural will, bringing it into obedience to a Universal principle and conferring subjective freedom. The East knew and to the present day knows only that *One* is free; the Greek and Roman world, that *some* are free; the German World knows that *All* are free.[4]

Hegel located the end of history in his 'German world' much in the same way as Fukuyama lodged the end of history in his 'America'. For both of them, their idea of 'freedom' is the yardstick for this triumph, as Hegel too, falsely identified a universal achievement as the prerogative of one nation. In the case of Fukuyama, the United States was a beacon of 'freedom'. In the case of Hegel it was thought to be Germany, as if nineteenth-century Europe or Prussia was a particularly free place for women, workers and minorities. Therefore, when Hegel likens the Orient in general to a childhood in history, when he argues that the 'religion of Islam . . . hates and proscribes everything concrete' and that 'its God is the absolute One, in relation to whom human beings retain for themselves no purpose, no private domain, nothing peculiar to themselves,'[5] the argument is the West has transcended the Orient, that humanity has overcome its original predicament, that the cycle of history from childhood to adolescence has left the 'East' at some infantile, underdeveloped stage. The 'white' man stands on its own feet as any adult does, whereas the rest of the world, including women, remain backward. Now that it has matured and left the rest of humankind behind, Western civilization is deemed timeless and universal. This is the perfect synthesis according to Hegel (and Fukuyama) – a singularity of history, that is erringly close to the ideas of those scientists that celebrate the arrival of Artificial General Intelligence, when machines are said to outdo us in pretty much any task.

---

[4]   Georg Wilhelm Friedrich Hegel, *The Philosophy of History*, New York: P.F. Collier & Son, 1902, emphasis added, p. 164.
[5]   Georg Wilhelm Friedrich Hegel, *Lectures on the Philosophy of Religion*, edited by Peter C. Hodgson and J. Michael Stewart, with the assistance of H.S. Harris, Berkeley: University of California Press, 1985, p. 243.

Technology and expansion

I think we can anchor the outward expansion of technology into every realm of society and our private space to this Enlightenment obsession with universal and infinite attributes of the seemingly Western experience. I doubt that Mark Zuckerberg or Bill Gates have read much of Hegel. So they must be unaware that their language and culture of thought, mirror some of the ideas that Hegel helped to shape. When Mark Zuckerberg speaks of universalizing Facebook into a global network in order to spread 'prosperity and freedom, promoting peace and understanding, lifting people out of poverty, and accelerating science', he is one step away from Hegel's teleological idea to bring about the end of all historical struggles, just that it would not be Germany that forces the Owl of Minerva to descend, but Facebook.

For Zuckerberg 'History is the story of how we've learned to come together in ever greater numbers – from tribes to cities to nations. Today we are close to taking our next step. Progress now requires humanity coming together not just as cities or nations', as Facebook 'stands for bringing us closer together and building [that] global community'.[6] The end of history, this time brought about by Facebook. The same ambition permeates the strategic statements of Bill Gates, as both Zuckerberg and Gates are very active as idea makers and as they both advance norms about equality, emancipation and other uniquely universal and timeless struggles, that their personal philanthropy also contributes to. Gates believes that

> We can make market forces work better for the poor if we can develop a more creative capitalism – if we can stretch the reach of market forces so that more people can make a profit, or at least make a living, serving people who are suffering from the worst inequities. We also can press governments around the world to spend taxpayer money in ways that better reflect the values of the people who pay the taxes. If we

---

6 'Mark Zuckerberg: Building a Global Community That Works for Everyone', *World Economic Forum*, 17 February 2017. Available at <https://www.weforum.org/agenda/2017/02/mark-zuckerberg-building-a-global-community-that-works-for-everyone/>.

can find approaches that meet the needs of the poor in ways that generate profits for business and votes for politicians, we will have found a sustainable way to reduce inequity in the world. This task is open-ended. It can never be finished. But a conscious effort to answer this challenge will change the world.[7]

There is nothing particularly wrong with these ideas in terms of their ethical content. Indeed, I think some of the personal attacks on Zuckerberg and Gates by conspiracy 'theorists' idiotic and vile. But if we read the two quotes above within the context of the Hegelian logic with which we started this chapter, they do reveal the meticulously global ambition of companies such as Facebook and Microsoft and the universalistic ethos that their technological logic is premised upon. Hence, Facebook, Microsoft, Google, Amazon, etc, are not merely profit-seeking companies. I have argued that they are part of a wider culture of thought that feeds into their mission statement and merges into an ideology that is distinctly expansionist, as it moves horizontally around the world and vertically, from the tech-giants to our living rooms and our very bodily functions. This amounts to what the genius Peruvian intellectual Aníbal Quijano called 'the coloniality of power' with reference to the systems of control, and hegemony that emerged in Europe during the modernist era.[8]

In order to disassemble this ideology further, it is easy to cross-reference the prolific French Philosopher Paulo Virilio who coined the term 'dromology', a neologism derived from the Latin word 'dromos' referring to a racecourse. In the research of Virilio, speed emerged as the main driving force of modern, Western societies, from the steam engine, the combustion engine, to our contemporary nuclear energy and immediate forms of drone warfare and global communication.[9]

---

7   'Remarks of Bill Gates: Harvard Commencement 2007', *The Harvard Gazette*, 7 June 2007. Available at <https://news.harvard.edu/gazette/story/2007/06/remarks-of-bill-gates-harvard-commencement-2007/>.

8   See further José Guadalupe Gandarilla, Salgado, María Haydeé García-Bravo, Daniel Benzi, 'Two decades of Aníbal Quijano's coloniality of power, Eurocentrism and Latin America,' *Contexto Internacional*, Vol. 43, No. 1 (2021), pp. 199–222

9   For a good compilation of his writings see James Der Derian (ed.), *The Virilio Reader*, Oxford: Blackwell, 1998.

However, Virilio passed away in 2018, perhaps right before the tech-giants peaked in their ability to mould society and politics. So for him it was still the military that emerges as the most powerful sector of society as it came to monopolize speed as a weapon of mass destruction. Yet today, the locus of this supersonic expansion is scattered, as it is the tech-companies that rush from one expansion to another, on a universal, teleological plane that neither Hegel nor Virilio could have fathomed. The velocity and trajectory of this technological machine is not merely remote, camouflaged by the secrecy that is typical for military institutions. Today – Jalal al-e Ahmad would not have been surprised – the machine is exactly microbial, atomistic, minute, as it attempts to penetrate every fibre of our body. Smart cities, wearable fitness and health sensors, children's toys and clothing that are interactive, technology constantly expands into our bodies, thus coding aspects of our behaviour. This bio-data is used by all major tech-companies to charter patterns of individual tastes and preferences and they feed into the algorithms employed for problematic methods such as psychometric profiling.

There are psychometric tests everywhere, now, for instance at Cambridge's prestigious Judge Business School where one of the tests – the Orpheus Business Personality Inventory (OBPI) – promises to define some of our main personality traits. For a fee of £25 at the time of writing, the test would assess 'Proficiency, Work Orientation, Patience, Fair-mindedness, Loyalty and Initiative'.[10] Noldus Information Technology, a company that specializes in 'behavioural research' offers comparable products. For instance, the Observer XT complete solution program codes 'behaviours accurately on a timeline, from one or multiple videos' and it allows you to include audio, integrate data modalities such as eye tracking or emotion data 'in order to visualize and analyze' the results in an integrated format.[11] Another product marketed as a solution to behavioural patterns is called TrackLab. It is based on Ultra-Wideband tracking which is 'used for behavioural

[10]   See 'The Psychometrics Centre', Cambridge Judge Business School. Available at <https://www.psychometrics.cam.ac.uk/services/psychometric-tests/OBPI>.
[11]   See 'The Observer XT'. Available at <https://www.noldus.com/observer-xt>.

research in various fields, such as psychology, education, consumer behaviour, wayfinding, healthcare … TrackLab customers studied social interactions in the classroom, children's spatial memory processes, or walking patterns in different hospital ward layouts'.[12]

So-called emotion recognition systems, which are dependent on face mapping, are increasingly used to scan a person's face using a 3D laser scanning system, and then project and manipulate Computer Generated Images (CGI graphics) onto the face in real time – a form of virtual and highly sophisticated stage make-up central to OMOTE a new Japanese technology.[13] But face mapping can also be used to 'read' our emotional state and to psychologically sort and categorize us. Such tests are not only increasingly used by employers. They are also prone to be misused for forms of social and racial profiling that are based on tainted algorithms, as discussed.

This is why the UN commissioned a report that included research into the 'use of emotion recognition systems by public authorities, for instance for singling out individuals for police stops or arrests or to assess the veracity of statements during interrogations'.[14] So tech-capitalism drives a new kind of expansion into our life-worlds that is entirely intimate, as it is premised to assess, code and reformulate our bodies and cognitive faculties. This is done not only in order to satisfy the profit margins that these companies are built upon, as Zuboff rightly focused on. The system works exactly because it is also lodged into a wider ideology that is typically hegemonic. In this way our right to be left alone, one of the principles of being free, has withered away quite dramatically. Today, your privacy is your power and to shield it is a form of resistance.

---

[12]   See 'Track Lab'. Available at <https://www.noldus.com/tracklab-human>.

[13]   In Japanese OMOTE refers to the face, or a mask. For an artistic implementation see 'OMOTE / Real-Time Face Tracking & Projection Mapping', *Labocine*. Available at <https://www.labocine.com/films/omote-real-time-face-tracking-and-projection-mapping>

[14]   'UN Urges Moratorium on Use of AI Threatening Human Rights', *The Irish Times*, 15 September 2021. Available at <https://www.irishnews.com/magazine/technology/2021/09/15/news/un-urges-moratorium-on-use-of-ai-threatening-human-rights-2449471/>

The Zombie App

We can move on with clear confidence about the argument of this chapter, now. I have suggested in the first part that at least since Hegel, there has developed a central discourse in and about the West that is concerned with the end of history for all humankind. If the Owl of Minerva finally descended in the West, as Hegel promised, the end of history was deemed possible. This grand idea of an end of history emerged out of the belief in the positively euphoric vision of the West's supreme evolution, itself a product of the methodical trust in the effectiveness of historical development that was central to the perspective of the Enlightenment. The tech-giants are a contemporary manifestation of this world-view.

The Hegelian methodology, albeit not all-encompassing, became a major pillar of Enlightenment thought. This was particularly the case for the human sciences, which have been continuously concerned with scientific evolution and perfection, especially from the eighteenth century onwards, as I have argued in the previous chapter. From then on the (European) human sciences continued to speculate about the transcendental. But instead of pursuing the utopia of God, they accentuated the utopia of science. It is out of this cultural habitat that the techno-utopian scientism of the tech-giants emerged.

There is another social-psychological angle to all of this that has been widely discussed by some of the rather more perceptive critical thinkers that we have. In several studies about the sense of life and the meaning of death, it has been rightly noted that the disenchantment from God, his proclaimed death that the Enlightenment prided itself upon, ushered in a very new pathology for humankind that was distinctly modern.[15] Whereas in the Middle Ages, before the dawn of atheism, death was associated with a godly ordained cycle of life, suddenly the separation from God compelled Enlightenment thinkers

---

[15]   See further Arshin Adib-Moghaddam, 'A (Short) History of the Clash of Civilisation', *Cambridge Review of International Affairs*, 21, No. 2 (June 2008), 217–234.

to rationalize the meaning of life without an after-life. What did it mean that we don't return to God anymore?

Since God has been considered the only way to make sense of life and the after-life, the modern mentality thus affected by his death, engendered a very particular fear of demise and physical ends. Life expectancy increased, infant mortality was contained, death was tamed and ghettoized in modern hospitals and a public health system that would organize and depersonalize dying by clearly separating it from the private realm, that is the family context within which people used to pass away. In short, the Enlightenment fostered a very particular obsession with extending life. If there was no after-life, if heaven and hell is here, then modern people needed to transcend this threat of finitude. A whole genre of 'horror' novels, from Mary Shelley's *Frankenstein* published in 1818 to Bram Stoker's *Dracula* published in 1897 spoke to this obsession with immortality.

My argument would be incomplete and unpersuasive could I not lodge this fear of death in some contemporary examples where AI technology attempts to 'play God', to extend our life-time. Again, there is no real value judgement involved in this particular section. I am merely demonstrating how we are still caught up in some of the ideas that dominated the *zeitgeist* of Enlightenment Europe. I will continue to make explicit their destructive legacies whenever the boundaries between good and bad are clear to me. But in terms of this obsession with cheating death, there is an interesting story about a recent patent that Microsoft registered in the United States' Patent and Trademark Office (USPTO). What could be referred to as the 'Zombie App', the programme would allow a chatbot to pose as a deceased friend or family member. In this way one of your loved ones could be digitally resurrected or reincarnated.[16]

---

[16] Isaiah Alonzo, 'Microsoft Chatbot Patent Aims to Bring the Dead Back to Life via Smartphone—Black Mirror?', *TechTimes*, 7 January 2021. Available at <https://www.techtimes.com/articles/255682/20210107/microsoft-chatbot-really-bring-back-dead-via-smartphone-new-patent.htm>.

Unsurprisingly, you would need to give the programmers access to all the sensitive and highly private information of the person's data and conversation history, for instance on Telegram, WhatsApp, Messenger or Signal. Eventually, the AI technology would enable a speech function that would let you talk to your dead loved one. The 'Zombie App' mirrors almost exactly the plot of the Netflix blockbuster series 'Black Mirror', apart from the detail that Microsoft has not speculated about – creating a humanoid with distinctly human qualities consoling a grieving widow, which was the plot of the series. Undoubtedly, the next step would be exactly that, however, as this technology can be easily synthesized with the burgeoning market for human-like robots, that could be uploaded with the dead person's personal data in order to mimic his/her speech patterns and preferences.

In Chapter 2, we have already talked about the 'immortality economy' and the 'Coalition for Radical Life Extension', which is a part of the 'youth' obsession in Silicon Valley, which will be quite apparent to anyone with some closer private or professional encounters there. The futurist Raymond Kurzweil has termed the ability to cheat death, 'escape velocity', when medical technology advances so spectacularly, that it will add more than a year each year, to our remaining life expectancy. This added time would allow us to outpace our own deaths.[17]

The idea of finding the elixir of youth, and to outdo death, is nothing new, of course. Neither is it limited to Europe. Cleopatra famously searched for eternal youth. In fact, the ancient Egyptians embalmed corpses turning them into mummies in order to preserve the eternal soul and to prepare for the after-life. The mighty Inca empire centred around Cuzco in Peru where the High Priest would reside, paid respect to Supay, the God of Death and the ruler of the underworld. They too would mummify their notables in order to prepare them for life after death.

---

[17] 'UN Urges Moratorium on Use of AI Threatening Human Rights', *Irish Times*, 15 September 2021. Available at <https://www.irishnews.com/magazine/technology/2021/09/15/news/un-urges-moratorium-on-use-of-ai-threatening-human-rights-2449471/>.

But today's immortality economy hasn't much to do with such spiritual ideas that associate death with an experience in the after-life. The immortality economy is steeped in the Enlightenment idea that everything is here. When there is no other-worldly realm, it is in this world that we can seek the 'Garden of Eden'. This amounts to an extremist Enlightenment obsession with eternal life. The upgrade to our this-worldly experience could only happen with the death of God and the destruction of what used to be associated as his realm. And perhaps it is this absence of the other-worldly that rationalizes the decision of today's futurists and life-expansion enthusiasts to freeze their bodies when they die, in anticipation that they would be resurrected in the future. There are senior philosophers, colleagues at some of the UK's most prestigious universities (though not that I know of at SOAS), who have signed up to such 'Cryonics Institutes'. So they wear tiny bands which would identify them to collaborating hospitals and which qualifies them to have their dead bodies' blood replaced with liquid nitrogen. The chain of such companies is ever expanding. The cheaper version allows you to freeze only your head. For the upgrade you could freeze your whole body. Today, therefore, the entanglement of the Enlightenment with hegemonic conquest – in this instance manifesting itself in the obsession with eternal life – is realized in the expansion of technology into the realm of death.

The softer version of this immortality economy is also called 'digital afterlife', an AI genre that was spearheaded by people in grief. For instance, Muhammad Aurangzeb Ahmad created one of the first chatbots when his father passed away, whereas Eugenia Kuda founded the highly successful 'companion APP' called Replika after her close friend died. The machine-learning algorithms behind the Replika chatbot are designed to mimic the type of deeper conversations we would have with family, close friends, partners or therapists. I have to admit that I found the APP inadequate and sterile and I wouldn't want to upload a deceased loved one on any digital platform based on that experience. The fact that variations of such chatbot applications that use natural-language processing (NLP) have been used to treat mental illnesses or diseases such as Dementia buttresses my argument for better regulation of the AI-sector. NLP may help to identify which parts of a dialogue between the client and the therapist are most effective at treating a variety of mental problems including post-traumatic disorder (PTSD) as computational psychologists, even the World Economic Forum suggest.[18] But NLP opens up a vast array of ethical questions that the present study has been flagging, certainly questions of race and gender as already indicated. In fact, very recent research has shown that algorithms continue to discriminate against minority populations, even if they are trained not to.[19] Undoubtedly, such discrimination must be particularly scrutinized in the mental health sector.

Data *Lebensraum*

We have established that spatial elements are always present in the West's own self-definition, at times in expansive terms and at others in conflictual, tragic, and obsessive ones. In this way, the European political tradition could pretend to cast its politics over the entire world, paradoxically, because it conceived of Europe as a finite horizon, exactly as the West, where sun set – *finis terrae*. Europe had to escape its own finitude and to conquer what the German political theorist Leopold von Ranke termed *Lebensraum*, a major concept in the politics of the nineteenth and early twentieth centuries. Thus was born the imperialist idea of expansion which has now a distinctly digital dimension, as we are embroiled in a new form of data geopolitics. Expansion, then, was inscribed into the idea of the West and it is also central to the conquest of our everyday lives by the so-called tech-giants.

---

[18] '4 Ways Artificial Intelligence Is Improving Mental Health Therapy', *World Economic Forum*, 22 December 2021. Available at <https://www.weforum.org/agenda/2021/12/ai-mental-health-cbt-therapy/>.

[19] Jingwei Li et al., 'Cross-Ethnicity/Race Generalization Failure of Behavioral Prediction from Resting-State Functional Connectivity', *Science Advances*, 8, No. 11 (2022). Available at <https://www.science.org/doi/10.1126/sciadv.abj1812>.

Post-colonial and/or 'decolonial' theorists have established, and the present study has tapped into some of their findings, that the imperial culture thus constituted is not unstructured or unsystematic. It is reflected in the discourse and institutional artefacts that the imperial projects informed, as Aníbal Quijano teaches us with his unique humanist brilliance. At least since the eighteenth century onwards, a whole new terminology designating regions was created in accordance with the interests of the imperial functionaries. Beyond it, there developed corresponding disciplines, at that time with a clearly pseudo-scientific agenda, e.g. Political Science, Anthropology, Geography, Area Studies and International Relations (IR) at a later stage. These disciplines were meant to systematically charter the world in order to make sense of it, to compartmentalize it, to make it available, analysable, and controllable. Imperial functionaries had to know where to go in order to get there and they had to learn to effectively control what they had already conquered.

The difference to spatial compartmentalizations in the Classical and Middle Ages was, that the emerging disciplinary apparatus was highly systematized, that it developed an internal coherence that embedded and extended the causal principle scientifically. Edward Said and others have linked these discourse-knowledge-power mutations to the Eurocentric mapping of the world. As indicated, the current digital map is equally 'Euro-Americo-centric.' At the time of writing only one Facebook data centre is not located in what is considered to be a Western country. Google has 14 data centres in the US, six in Europe, one in Chile, and one each in Singapore and Taiwan.[20] As Couldry and Mejas rightly established: These 'data relations enact a new form of data colonialism, normalizing the exploitation of human beings through data, just as historic colonialism appropriated territory and resources and ruled subjects for profit.'[21]

---

[20] Google's data centre locations can be accessed here <https://www.google.com/about/datacenters/locations/>.
[21] Nick Couldry and Ulises A. Mejias, 'Data Colonialism: Rethinking Big Data's Relation to the Contemporary Subject', *Television & New Media*, 20, No. 4 (2019), p. 336.

Furthermore, at least since the terrorist attacks on the United States on 11 September 2001, the intelligence and military agencies in the country and the tech-giants, in particular Google, have converged closely in their interest to organize and make accessible global information flows for the purpose of surveillance, control and military warfare. When in April 2017, the Pentagon asked Google to clandestinely advance an AI-powered tool that could identify targets in drone footage, it provoked a spirited revolt against building weapons, but it also revealed the increasing collaboration between the military and the tech-world. 'We believe that Google should not be in the business of war,' more than 3,000 Google employees wrote in April 2021 to company CEO Sundar Pichai that prompted other colleagues to follow and for Pichai to shelve Google's participation in this particular project.[22] The program dubbed 'Project Maven' was meant to identify objects from video footage, using algorithms, which could then be singled out by troops as potential targets. As the head of the Department of Defence's Algorithmic Warfare Cross-Function team said: 'Project Maven focuses on computer vision – an aspect of machine learning and deep learning – that autonomously extracts objects of interest from moving or still imagery'. He made it crystal clear that 'we are in an AI arms race ... It's happening in industry [and] the big five Internet companies are pursuing this heavily. Many of you will have noted that Eric Schmidt [executive chairman of Alphabet Inc.] is calling Google an AI company now, not a data company.'[23]

Not unlike some of the social science disciplines that were caught up in traditional forms of imperial domination during the Enlightenment, today's technology is meant to make available the non-Western world, if necessary for military domination. 'No area will be left unaffected by

---

22   For the letter see "The Business of War': Google Employees Protest Work for the Pentagon', *The New York Times*, 4 April 2018. Available at <https://www.nytimes.com/2018/04/04/technology/google-letter-ceo-pentagon-project.html>.

23   'Project Maven to Deploy Computer Algorithms to War Zone by Year's End', *US Department of Defense*, 21 July 2017. Available at <https://www.defense.gov/News/News-Stories/Article/Article/1254719/project-maven-to-deploy-computer-algorithms-to-war-zone-by-years-end/>.

the impact of this technology', it is typically proclaimed by intelligence officials.[24] So it does not come as a surprise, that senior US military personnel are on the record for saying that programs such as Project Maven are trialled in the 'Middle East' and Africa where data is pulled from ScanEagle drones that operate in Iraq, as well as larger Predator and Reaper drones. As one of the strategic thinkers in this field, Lt. Col. Garry Floyd said at a major technology conference: 'We're in five or six locations in AFRICOM and CENTCOM . . . Data is like iron ore, there's mountains of it'.[25]

Unsurprisingly, Lt. Floyd is a great admirer of Carl von Clausewitz (1780–1831), another major Enlightenment figure and someone who was influenced by Hegel's dialectical methodology. The Prussian general is a must read at most US military academies. Writing in the *Strategic Studies Quarterly*, Floyd argues that the 'world is wired with networks and unblinking sensors that track everything from spending habits to the movements of armies'.[26] Within this fast moving and complex data world, Floyd identifies what he calls the 'attribution advantage' as a strategic goal to thwart 'nonattributable' activity, which 'might include covert aerial drone strikes, difficult-to-trace offensive cyberattacks, special operations forces operating deep in another country, or information attacks designed to undermine rival governments'.[27] At the time of writing the article, Floyd was a senior member of the Algorithmic Warfare Cross Functional Team within the Office of the US Undersecretary of Defense for Intelligence. Most of the data feeding into the practical application of such theories is currently gathered in sub-Saharan Africa and Iraq without much governmental scrutiny in the countries concerned.

[24] Ibid., and 'Google Wants to Make Military Spy Drones Even Smarter', *Live Science*, 7 March 2018. Available at <https://www.livescience.com/61952-google-providing-ai-drone-footage-department-of-defense.html>.

[25] 'Pentagon's Big AI Program, Maven, Already Hunts Data in Middle East, Africa', *Breaking Defense*, 1 May 2018. Available at <https://breakingdefense.com/2018/05/pentagons-big-ai-program-maven-already-hunts-data-in-middle-east-africa/>.

[26] Lt Col Garry S. Floyd Jr, 'Attribution and Operational Art: Implications for *Competing in Time*', *Strategic Studies Quarterly*, 12, No. 2 (2018), p. 17.

[27] Ibid., 19–20.

Data wars

Today the synergy between the tech-giants and what used to be the military-industrial complex furthers an almost messianic zeal to layer the world with narratives of freedom and neo-liberal transparency, which makes access to data (and other resources) that much easier. Today's data imperialists connect neatly with the ideal of the liberal state and its universal mission to safeguard and export 'justice' and 'civilization'. For John Stuart Mill (1806–1873), for instance, another doyen of the European Enlightenment, the just cause of the British Empire to civilize other nations justified the means, if necessary to conquer 'barbarous neighbours' or 'to break their spirit' until they 'gradually sink into a state of dependence'.[28]

We have already established that the ideas of nation, people, civilization and racial superiority are never very far apart. But Mill's mode of argumentation was not reliant on the issue of race, at least not explicitly. What Mill defended was the suspension of the national sovereignty of the 'other', i.e. uncivilized nations. He was denying them the opportunity to turn the sovereignty principle on the West itself. In this sense, national sovereignty was deemed a prerogative of the civilized nations of Europe. 'To suppose that the same international customs, and the same rules of international morality, can obtain between one civilised nation and another, and between civilised nations and barbarians', Mill clearly argued, 'is a grave error, and one which no statesmen can fall into'.[29] If Britain was the carrier of a higher cause, it was obliged to enforce its values globally, if necessary by force. This is the central premise of the modern 'liberal-crusader state' that is the product of European imperialisms in the eighteenth and nineteenth centuries. It arrogates to itself the mission to export liberty and freedom

---

[28] John Stuart Mill, *Dissertations and Discussions: Political, Philosophical and Historical*, Vol. 3, London: Longmans, Green, Reader, and Dyer, 1867, 168–169.
[29] Ibid., p. 167.

to those less fortunate peoples, who are presumed to suffer under the yoke of their own backwardness.[30]

For those of you who still believe that these connections are too far fetched, I'd like to present another recent example for the extension of the new data *Lebensraum* in the spirit of suspending the sovereignty of other nations, as Mill and other Enlightenment thinkers clearly defended. In March 2018, multiple media outlets reported that a British firm called Cambridge Analytica had acquired and used the personal data of up to 87 million Facebook users. They were able to do this via the approximately 270,000 Facebook users who used the App 'This is your digital life'.[31] The users of this third-party App made the mistake to give their consent to their data usage, that provided the App with access to data from the user's contact networks. Facebook quickly banned 'This is your digital life' from its servers and severed its ties with Cambridge Analytica, once the scandal hit the newsstands.

No wonder then that Cambridge Analytica also supported the re-election of Donald Trump by segmenting US society in terms of carefully calibrated psycho-political profiles (e.g. core, susceptible or engaged supporter of the candidates) in order to target them with the firm's invasive data propaganda.[32] This was made technologically viable through the predictive data analytics provided by Facebook's FBLearner Flow machine intelligence. There was a racial component geared to voter suppression, too, as Cambridge Analytica's data strategy included the attempt to persuade African-American voters in key swing states to

---

[30]   On 'significant others' and the way they informed Europe's collective identity formation, see also Iver B. Neumann, *Uses of the Other: 'The East' in European Identity Formation*, Minneapolis: University of Minnesota Press, 1999, and Michael Patrick Cullinane and David Ryan (eds.), *U.S. Foreign Policy and the Other*, Oxford: Berghahn, 2014.

[31]   See Cecilia Kang and Sheera Frenkel, 'Facebook says Cambridge Analytica Harvested Data of up to 87 Million Users', *The New Work Times*, 4 April 2018. Available at <https://www.nytimes.com/2018/04/04/technology/mark-zuckerberg-testify-congress.html>, and Alex Hern, 'How to Check Whether Facebook Shared Your Data with Cambridge Analytica', The Guardian, 10 April 2018. Available at <https://www.theguardian.com/technology/2018/apr/10/facebook-notify-users-data-harvested-cambridge-analytica>.

[32]   On the nexus between data and the challenge to democracy see among others Stephanie Hankey, Julianne Kerr Morrison and Ravi Naik, 'Data and Age Democracy in the Digital', report by The Constitution Society, London 2018.

boycott the vote, which would have favoured the election campaign of Donald Trump. The database singled out 3.5 million African-Americans into a psycho-profiled category that was termed 'Deterrence', in order to micro-target them for messages designed to dissuade them from voting.[33]

But the story doesn't end there. Some of the data acquired by Cambridge Analytica was used to influence elections all over the world and in particular in formerly colonized countries in Africa. With reference to the re-election of Kenyan President Uhuru Kenyatta in 2013 and 2017 – which was mired in civil unrest and violence and which was aided and abetted by targeted political advertising enabled by Cambridge Analytica – a former employee of the company said that Cambridge Analytica 'goes around the world and undermines civic institutions of, you know, countries that are struggling to develop those institutions'. Cambridge Analytica was seen as 'an example of what modern day colonialism looks like. You have a wealthy company from a developed nation going into an economy or democracy that is still struggling to get, you know, its feet on the ground and taking advantage of that to profit from that'.[34]

Further evidence revealed by an undercover sting organized by the British broadcaster Channel 4 demonstrated that Cambridge Analytica successfully supported the re-election of Kenyan President Uhuru Kenyatta's in 2013 and 2017. 'We have rebranded the entire party twice, written their manifesto, done two rounds of 50,000 (participant) surveys,' Mark Turnbull, managing director of Cambridge Analytica Political Global, admitted in the undercover footage. 'Then we'd write all the speeches and we'd stage the whole thing – so just about every element of his campaign'.[35]

---

[33] See 'Cambridge Analytica Database Identified Black Voters as Ripe for "Deterrence," British Broadcaster Says', *The Washington Post*, 28 September 2020. Available at <https://www.washingtonpost.com/context/cambridge-analytica-database-disproportionately-identified-black-voters-as-ripe-for-deterrence/127e78d6-03c2-4b3f-8675-2d7e14c4b528/?itid=lk_inline_manual_9>.

[34] 'Exposed: Undercover Secrets of Trump's Data Firm', *Channel 4 News*, 20 March 2018. Available at <https://www.channel4.com/news/exposed-undercover-secrets-of-donald-trump-data-firm-cambridge-analytica>.

[35] Ibid.

Sovereignty, democracy and elections for sale. This gives the present chapter the title 'Techno-imperialism'. It connects with my overarching argument, that some of the nefarious legacies of the European Enlightenment continue to haunt our AI-driven digital world. We all know that Cambridge Analytica closed operations in 2018. But the geopolitical war over our data continues unabated. Just as I am writing these lines, the UK-based AI start up Faculty raised US$42.5 million in a growth funding round. The company was instrumental in winning the Brexit vote for the UK Leave campaign. A private company aptly called 'Dynamic Maps' owned and controlled by Dominic Cummings, the mastermind behind the campaign for the election of the former British Prime Minister Boris Johnson, paid more than a quarter of a million pounds to Faculty which worked on the Vote Leave campaign by targeting voters on social media sites, in particular on Facebook.[36]

Faculty has also been telling global corporates like Red Bull and Virgin Media what to suggest to their customers, based on the processing of vast amounts of data. Targeted advertisement for political purposes used to be called propaganda, as it is meant to warp the truth in favour of a political movement and/or agenda. In this case Faculty used their AI know-how to flood Facebook users with pro-Brexit messages. At the height of the Coronavirus crisis, Faculty won a foothold in the most coveted area in the geopolitics of data. i.e. the health sector. Faculty was awarded a contract with NHSX, which employed the company's services to help develop the Covid-19 Data Store as part of its work with the NHSX AI Lab. The platform uses NHS data to calibrate the national response to the pandemic and to anticipate potential crisis areas. A report by Britain's National Audit Office revealed that a cabinet minister in the UK government owned £90,000 shares in Faculty when it was awarded the £2.3m contract from NHSX to help organize the NHS Covid-19 Data Store.[37] The geopolitics of data, then, is real and it is a major battlefield of contemporary politics.

---

[36] 'Revealed: Dominic Cummings Firm paid Vote Leave's AI Firm £260,000', *The Guardian*, 12 July 2020, Available at <https://www.theguardian.com/politics/2020/jul/12/revealed-dominic-cummings-firm-paid-vote-leaves-ai-firm-260000>.

[37] 'Cabinet Minister Owned £90,000 Shares in Faculty at Time of NHSX Contract', *Digital Health*, 18 November 2020. Available at <https://www.digitalhealth.net/2020/11/cabinet-minister-owned-90000-shares-in-faculty-at-time-of-nhsx-contract/>.

5

Death-Techniques

I ended the last chapter with another fragment of my argument: I tried to show that imperial expansion during the Enlightenment was justified on the basis of historical and racial norms in order to demonstrate why techno-imperialism is equally charged with such dubious notions such as 'civilization' and 'expansion'. Moreover, I continued to argue that the supersonic, microbial reach of technology into our everyday life has eroded our individual sovereignty challenging our hard-earned ability to be free, or at least to indulge in the freedom to be left alone, unbothered by the digital world and its constant demands on online participation and virtual 'community'.

The second point that I made is that techno-imperialism is not only about the geopolitics of data or surveillance capitalism. Not unlike traditional forms of imperialism, the expansion of the 'Matrix' everywhere (including into space) is enveloped by an ideology that accentuates the neo-liberal mantra of access and accessibility. The spatial organization of the world that used to be the purview of the traditional social sciences of the Enlightenment has transmuted into the geopolitics of data exactly because bio-power can be exercised everywhere now. All of this transcends and challenges sovereignty, from the individual's ability to be autonomous, to the ability of some nation-states to control their electoral processes. The becoming of techno-imperialism is geopolitical in this exact way.

The self-proclaimed mission to connect the world that is so central to Facebook, Twitter and other prominent social media sites opens up a varied tool box to exercise and legitimate hegemony. In this regard, the tech-giants connect quite directly to the imperial discourses of the past, sometimes implicitly when Mark Zuckerberg speaks of the next step of social development brought about by the globalizing and universalizing prospect of his Metaverse or rather explicitly when the founder and CEO of the space exploration company SpaceX and Tesla, Elon Musk, defends a coup d'état in Bolivia, which has one of the world's largest reserves of Lithium, an essential component in the battery systems that make Tesla cars run. 'We will coup whoever we want. Deal with it!', Musk tweeted in response to the accusation that the US government was supporting right-wing fascists to oust the democratically elected socialist President of Bolivia, Evo Morales.[1] In the end, the Bolivian people – and here in particular the indigenous communities on whose lands Lithium is mined – 'dealt with it' indeed. They reinstated the party of Morales reversing the coup d'état that Musk had defended.

Musk has bought Twitter in the name of 'civilization' and as a self-avowed 'free speech absolutist', probably unaware that these are typically imperial planks that have been used to subjugate entire cultures, that is both economically and discursively.[2] This language received a response from the global Hacktivist group 'Anonymous:' 'Recently... people are beginning to see you as another narcissistic rich dude who is desperate for attention ... It appears that your quest to save the world is more rooted in a superiority complex than it is in actual concern for humanity.'[3]

Such criticism may seem harsh to many, in particular as Musk has supported resistance struggles that align with the anti-hegemonic goals of Anonymous. For instance in Ukraine, where Musk donated Starlink internet packages after the invasion of the country by Russia in February 2022. With the right 'kit', that is satellite-based internet terminals, Starlink ensures access to the internet for everyone, everywhere circumventing censorship by governments, if necessary. At the time of

[1]   'After Bolivia, Elon Musk Says Capitalists Can Overthrow Any Government They Want', *People's World*, 27 July 2020. Available at <https://www.peoplesworld.org/article/after-bolivia-elon-musk-says-capitalists-can-overthrow-any-government-they-want/>.
[2]   'Will Elon Musk Be the 'Free Speech Absolutist Twitter Needs?', *Breitbart*, 14 April 2022. Available at <https://www.breitbart.com/politics/2022/04/14/nolte-will-elon-musk-be-the-free-speech-absolutist-twitter-needs/>.
[3]   'Anonymous Calls out "Narcissistic Rich Dude" Elon Musk', *Dazed*, 6 June 2021. Available at <https://www.dazeddigital.com/science-tech/article/53080/1/anonymous-calls-out-narcissistic-rich-dude-elon-musk-cryptocurrency-bitcoin>.

writing, the US has sent more than 15,000 Starlink kits to Ukraine, as Ukraine's government worked closely with the US to import terminals and maintain internet infrastructure.

Furthermore, in September 2022, the US Treasury Department issued guidance on expanding internet services available to Iranians, despite US sanctions on the country.[4] This came after Musk tweeted that he would make Starlink available to Iranians in support of demonstrations for women's rights, which were violently suppressed by the hardline government of President Ebrahim Raisi. In Iran, too, Anonymous and Musk seemed to be on the same side, as the former hacked several Iranian government and state-affiliated media websites in a concerted cyber-attack.[5] The difference to Elon Musk is of course, that Anonymous is a not a for-profit organization and does not have ties to the US state or any other state for that matter. As a matter of fact, in August 2022, Musk's SpaceX company launched a 'top secret US spy satellite' under the US National Security Space Launch mission.[6] US allies benefit, too. In June 2022, SpaceX launched a military radar satellite for the German government and the company has signed a contract with South Korea to launch five spy satellites until 2025.[7] In the case of Musk, there is at least convergence with US foreign policies, certainly in the cases that I have surveyed for this study.

Technology, then, can be a major 'sovereignty buster' not only in our everyday lives but also in world politics. The comprehensive intrusion

[4] 'U.S. Treasury Hints Elon Musk's SpaceX Can Export Internet Equipment to Iran', *The Foreign Desk*, 22 September 2022. Available at <https://foreigndesknews.com/top-story/u-s-treasury-says-elon-musks-spacex-can-export-internet-equipment-to-iran/>.

[5] '"Anonymous" Hacks Iran State Websites after Mahsa Amini's Death', *MBB News*, 22 September 2022. Available at <https://mbbnews.me/anonymous-hacks-iran-state-websites-after-mahsa-aminis-death/>.

[6] Kate Duffy, 'SpaceX will launch top secret US spy satellites with the reusable Falcon Heavy rocket now that it's received Space Force approval, report says', *Business Insider*, 12 August 2022. Available at <https://www.businessinsider.com/elon-musk-spacex-launch-secret-spy-satellites-space-force-government-2022-8?r=US&IR=T>.

[7] See Stephen Clark, 'SpaceX launches German military radar satellite from California', *Spaceflight Now*, 18 June 2022. Available at <https://spaceflightnow.com/2022/06/18/spacex-launches-german-military-radar-satellite-from-california/>, and Park Si-soo, 'South Korea hires SpaceX to launch five spy satellites by 2025', *Space News*, 11 April 2022. Available at <https://spacenews.com/south-korea-hires-spacex-to-launch-five-spy-satellites-by-2025/>.

into our privacy is fairly novel compared to the Enlightenment, but comparably abusive. This 'merum imperium' aspect of the battle over digital/technological AI supremacy in contemporary world politics, falls neatly into the Enlightenment traditions of colonialism and imperialism or the coloniality of power that we pinpointed with the help of Quijano's theory among others. The tech-companies colonize our data and extract what they need from us in a truly expansionist fashion. In this chapter, I will focus on this issue more specifically. These new technologies enable governments to launch invisible wars that are fought beyond international law and normative/ethical restraints demanded by many of us. Therefore, the production of unseen wars is yet another dangerous impact of technology. Today, governments do not invade with armies. They invade from nowhere: A drone attack, malware/ransomware invasion, a cyber-assault. All of that is happening beneath the veil of algorithmic unaccountability, if necessary.

The killing of the Iranian General Qasem Soleimani is probably the most prominent example for the death techniques that are possible today and for the abrogation of international law. Whether one likes Soleimani, or any other unlawfully targeted person for that matter, is secondary here. If we are to kill whoever we dislike, we may all become a target. It would also be right to interject that wars have always licensed the killing of individuals. But drone warfare in particular affords the state with a sanitized, remote and almost aestheticized version of warfare, that incorporates the individual in the act of killing, either as the target for whom the drone is assembled and programmed in the first place, or the executioner who pulls the trigger bringing about this death from above. My point is an analytical one as the norms of *jus ad bellum* (justice in going to war) and *jus in bello* (justice in the conduct of war), that had been conceptualized by legalists and IR scholars in order to rationalize traditional forms of warfare, have been practically suspended in these invisible wars in order to circumvent questions of sovereignty and accountability. In this way technology is not innocent. Indeed, it has become a harbinger of a neo-imperial death-technique that has liberated the machine to wage wars independent of our verdict.

The case of Soleimani that I present as a detailed excursus written in narrative style, is a case in point for this violent 'technosis'. His killing is an example for the technological frenzy that is aided and abetted by the tech-giants and which is an extension of the imperial logic of the Enlightenment and its sovereignty-busting mechanisms. Ultimately, that is my contention in the following paragraphs.

Death by remote control

3 January 2020 – A sunny day in Florida. President Trump is busy playing golf at the West Palm Beach Club. Hours before his break, an MQ-9 Reaper drone was instructed to kill General Qasem Soleimani, the most senior commander of Iran's elite Islamic Revolutionary Guard Corps (IRGC). All that was left behind, from the impact of the drone, was a pile of charred debris. If you could stomach to focus more deeply on the gruesome images, you could see a hand with a ruby ring – Soleimani's characteristic adornment.

The decision to kill Soleimani was made at Trump's Mar-a-Lago oceanfront residence, which he likes to refer to as the 'Winter White House'. Surrounded by Secretary of State Mike Pompeo, Defence Secretary Mark Esper, Chairman of the Joint Chiefs of Staff Mark Milley, acting White House chief of staff Mick Mulvaney, national security adviser Robert O'Brien and Legislative Affairs Director Eric Ueland, Trump was presented with a range of options for how to respond to escalating violence against US targets in Iraq, including striking Iranian ships and missile facilities or to target Iran's allies, in particular the Katai'b Hezbollah movement, whose Secretary-General Abu Mahdi al-Muhandis was eventually killed together with Soleimani.

Later on Trump would recall how he monitored the strikes from the White House Situation Room: 'They said, "Sir, and this is from, you know, cameras that are miles in the sky. They are together sir. Sir, they have two minutes and 11 seconds. No bullshit. They have two minutes and 11 seconds to live, sir. They're in the car. They're in an armored vehicle going. Sir, they have approximately one minute to live, sir. . . 30 seconds, 10, nine, eight. . . then all of a sudden boom. They're gone, sir."[8]

In the chaotic days leading to the assassinations, Pentagon officials gave Trump a range of options. Assassinating Soleimani was thought to be the most extreme of them, and no one really seemed to think he would take it. None of the Presidents before him considered killing a general of a sovereign state with no declaration of war. President George W. Bush had the option in the aftermath of 9/11 and the wars in Afghanistan and Iraq, and he didn't choose it. After all, the last time a US government ordered the killing of a major military official on foreign territory was during World War II, when the US military shot down a Japanese plane carrying admiral Isoroku Yamamoto. But that was after Pearl Harbour, when the US was officially at war with Imperial Japan. Today, with the availability of the new technologies, death could be brought about by remote control, and without much immediate, legal repercussion.

Soleimani himself was ordered to return to Baghdad, and with urgency due to the increasing tensions between the United States and Iran's allies among the Popular Mobilization Forces (PMF). The PMF is a part of the military establishment in Iraq. It acts as an umbrella organization that is composed of mostly Shia militias, but also includes members of the other communities, such as Sunni Muslims, Christians, Yazidis and more. On 2 January 2020 pro-Iranian militia members and demonstrators besieged the US embassy in Baghdad's Green Zone. A week earlier, a US civilian translator was killed and several US troops were wounded in a rocket attack on an Iraqi military base in Kirkuk. Although the PMF denied responsibility, the Trump administration accused them, and by extension Iran. The US responded with airstrikes on headquarters near the western al-Qa'im district on the border with Syria that killed 25 fighters of the Katai'b Hezbollah brigade, which is closely allied with Iran. Mike Pompeo trumpeted loudly from Trump's

---

8   'Timeline of Trump's Shifting Justifications for Soleimani Killing', *Al Jazeera*, 19 February 2020. Available at <https://www.aljazeera.com/news/2020/2/19/timeline-of-trumps-shifting-justifications-for-soleimani-killing>.

Mar-a-Lago club where he and Defence Secretary Esper had already gathered: 'We will not stand for the Islamic Republic of Iran to take actions that put American men and women in jeopardy'.[9]

On 3 January 2020, Soleimani entered a powder keg. When he arrived at Baghdad International Airport, the Reaper drones already had him in sight when his plane landed. The MQ-9 sometimes called predator B is the first so-called 'hunter killer' Unmanned Aerial Vehicle (UAV) designed for long-endurance, high-altitude surveillance. It quite literally was made to bring about death from the shadows. The aircraft is equipped with a high-definition camera and software to enable automatic detection of threats and tracking of 12 moving targets at once. It can fire 'super ripple' missiles within 0.32 seconds of each other.

Flight number 6Q 501 operated by the privately owned Cham Wings Airlines of Syria was delayed from Damascus by nearly three hours, most likely in order to confirm that Soleimani was actually on board. To that end, there must have been intelligence assets, at least at the Syrian airport and on the Airbus 320 itself. Flight 6Q 501 took off towards Baghdad with 156 passengers. There were 11 passengers in the front: five Iraqis and five Iranians, plus one Syrian passenger. In addition, there were five crew members, two pilots and four security personnel on board. In recent years, Soleimani was less cautious while travelling, but he still made sure to do so with passengers in order to deflect from his position. His name didn't appear on any boarding pass, of course, but the US military was waiting for him.

The three MQ-9 Reaper Drones entered the Iraqi airspace at various times: 10:30 am, 11:30 am and at 3 pm in the afternoon. At Baghdad International Airport, the air traffic control tower recorded them as observatory drones only, not employed for military purposes. The skies of Baghdad are frequently swamped by these technologies of control and destruction, so they didn't raise any suspicion and kept circulating for several hours. At 12:33 am, traffic control confirmed the landing of

---

9 'US Attacks Iran-backed Militia Bases in Iraq and Syria', *BBC News*, 30 December 2019. Available at <https://www.bbc.com/news/world-middle-east-50941693>.

Soleimani's flight. The Al-Cham airplane touched down on the runway facing Gate 33 in the Samara arrivals terminal. A few minutes later, the doors of the airplane opened and the passengers started to disembark.

At the same time two vehicles entered the K1 gate, which is designated for cargo, at least one of them a saloon car to accommodate Soleimani's entourage. The two vehicles parked closely by the plane on the tarmac. Mohammed Rida al-Jaberi, an officer in the PMF, got off and climbed on board the aircraft. Soleimani was the last to disembark wearing a face mask and hat to conceal himself. Abu Mahdi al-Muhandis, the deputy commander of the Katai'b Hezbollah force and a long-time comrade and friend of Soleimani, was waiting for him in one of the vehicles.

The convoy made its way from the cargo area exit. They passed through a tunnel, which leads to the main airport road within what is known as the security fence within Baghdad International Airport, heading towards the eastern exit. On the right-hand side of the road there was the security fence and on the left the main facilities of the airport. Trump and his team were briefed about the events from his hideout in sunny Florida. CIA Director Gina Haspel was observing from the headquarters of the agency in Langley, Virginia and Secretary of Defense Mark Esper was following the events from another remote location. The operation itself was conducted from US Central Command (CENTCOM) forward headquarters in Qatar, which explains why the Qatari Emir Tamim Bin Hamad Al Thani travelled to Tehran immediately after the killing to de-escalate the situation, as Doha enjoys close relations with both the US and Iran. The whole operation, then, could only function because distance between the trigger point and the target was minimized by various camouflaged combat technologies.

The point of explosion was 100 metres before the airport's western exit. The remote team operating the drones decided to pull the trigger before the convoy exited the premises and mingled with the traffic in Baghdad. The drones targeted the vehicles using three hellfire missiles killing everyone. The CIA had developed the Hellfire R9x in 2019. Instead of an explosive warhead, it is equipped with six spring-loaded steel blades which pop out in all directions just before impact which may explain the gruesome images of Soleimani's severed hand, and the pile of debris, rather than a mere crater. These technologies are developed to kill efficiently. Here, as well, access and accessibility are key factors. In this case, they were meant to kill with ease.

The bladed killing machine is dubbed 'Flying Ginsu' among the US intelligence community and war-technology enthusiasts named after the kitchen knives that were made famous among US housewives due to a wave of commercials from the late 1970s onwards. The right-wing press celebrated this new 'Ninja bomb', 'knife missile' and 'bladed anvil' which 'minces' and 'shreds' the enemies of the United States to death when it was used against al-Qaeda leaders in 2019.[10] The missiles only weigh 45 kilograms each. Yet, the kinetic energy unleashed upon impact promises a 100 per cent lethal danger zone of 76 cm which is enough to kill anyone within the immediate range of the blades.

And so it did. Apart from Soleimani and al-Muhandis, there were several other casualties including Major General Hossein Pourjafari, a friend of Soleimani in the IRGC intelligence wing, who hailed from the same province and who had been close to him since the Iran–Iraq war, both as an advisor and his security guard. Colonel Shahroud Mozaffari-Nia was another Iran–Iraq war veteran; he operated primarily in Lebanon and Syria. Lieutenant Hadi Taremi was Soleimani's number one bodyguard and a fellow member of the elite Quds force. Lieutenant Vahid Zamanian was only 27 years old; he made his career in the Basij-e Mostazafin, a volunteer paramilitary group subordinated to the IRGC. Muhammad Rida al-Jabri was an airport protocol officer for the PMF and he was accompanied by three additional members of the PMF who were acting as bodyguards.

The three drones that ended the lives of these men, left the airspace seven minutes after the attack. Three US military jets then entered

---

[10] 'The CIA's Blade-Wielding "Flying Ginsu" Missile Strikes Again', *Popular Mechanics*, 10 December 2019. Available at <https://www.popularmechanics.com/military/weapons/a30175425/cia-blade-missile/>.

instead. Air traffic control warned them and tried to convince them to leave as they were in clear violation of Iraqi airspace. Two left but the third remained. The rather unassuming and low-key operation showed that the US had been tracking Soleimani for months. The US must have gathered intelligence from all the organizations that Soleimani traversed – the Syrian Army, the Quds Force in Damascus, Hezbollah in Damascus, the Damascus and Baghdad airports and Katai'b Hezbollah and Popular Mobilization forces in Iraq – to track his movements. Just on New Year's Day, Soleimani had met with the leader of the Lebanese Hezbollah movement, Hassan Nasrallah. Nasrallah was worried about the high profile of Soleimani and warned his good friend that his life was in danger. Soleimani laughed and replied as he did on many occasions in his life, stressing that he hoped to die as a martyr and asking Nasrallah to pray that he would. At 5:25 am on the morning of the assassination, the PMU confirmed the killing of al-Muhandis and Soleimani, followed by an announcement by the IRGC at 5:37 am.

It wasn't me

It wasn't until 9:46 p.m. on Thursday, 9 January that the US government officially confirmed Soleimani's death. In a hasty, 163-word Pentagon press release emailed to the favourite reporters of the White House it was stated: 'At the direction of the President, the U.S. military has taken decisive defensive action to protect U.S. personnel abroad by killing Qasem Soleimani, the head of the Islamic Revolutionary Guard Corps-Quds Force, a U.S.-designated Foreign Terrorist Organization.'[11]

It came out later that the only entity that knew about the assassination was the Israeli government of Prime Minister Netanyahu, which didn't come as a surprise to most of us with an understanding of US foreign

---

[11]   'Statement by the Department of Defense', *U.S. Department of Defense*, 2 January 2020. Available   at   <https://www.defense.gov/News/Releases/Release/Article/2049534/statement-by-the-department-of-defense/>.

policies in the region. It is notable that not even the US congress was notified, but Netanyahu was.

In the aftermath of the killing, the Trump administration scrambled for reasons to justify the assassination. On the day of the drone attack, Trump tweeted that 'General Qassem Soleimani has killed or badly wounded thousands of Americans over an extended period of time, and was plotting to kill many more ... but got caught!' In typically, hyperbolic fashion, the same Tweet made Soleimani 'directly and indirectly responsible for the death of millions of people'.[12] Trump addressed reporters from Mar-a-Lago on the same day, reiterating that Soleimani was 'plotting imminent and sinister attacks on American diplomats and military personnel, but we caught him in the act and terminated him'. The idea that Soleimani was in Iraq to plot an imminent attack on US assets was reconfirmed by Pompeo who alleged that Soleimani was 'actively plotting in the region to take actions, a big action ... that would have put dozens if not hundreds of American lives at risk'.[13]

During the following days, the contradictions piled up. At a White House event Trump said that he ordered the killing 'because they were looking to blow up our [Baghdad] embassy'. Yet on the same day Pompeo conceded that they 'don't know precisely when, where' that imminent attack would have happened. A day later Pompeo reiterated: 'I can reveal that I believe it would have been four embassies. And I think that probably Baghdad already started ... could have been military bases, could have been a lot of other things too. But it was imminent and then all of a sudden, he was gone.'[14]

On the CBS programme, Adam Schiff created even more doubts about the official narrative, saying that there was no discussion in the

[12] 'Qasem Soleimani: US Kills Top Iranian General in Baghdad Air Strike', *BBC News*, 3 January 2020. Available at <https://www.bbc.com/news/world-middle-east-50979463>.

[13] 'Secretary Michael R. Pompeo With John Berman of CNN New Day', *U.S. Department of State*, 3 January 2020. Available at <https://2017-2021.state.gov/secretary-michael-r-pompeo-with-john-berman-of-cnn-new-day/index.html>.

[14] Eugene Kiely, 'Trump Administration's Shifting Statements on Soleimani's Death', *FactCheck.org*, 15 January 2020. Available at <https://www.factcheck.org/2020/01/trump-administrations-shifting-statements-on-soleimanis-death/>.

briefings that 'these are the four embassies being targeted'.[15] The idea
that an imminent attack on four embassies was the casus belli for the
decision to assassinate Soleimani and that there was conclusive
intelligence to that end was undermined by Defence Secretary Mark
Esper a couple of days later. He admitted that he 'didn't see' intelligence
confirming that four embassies were being targeted. Instead, according
to Esper, he thought Trump was relaying his belief that they 'could have
been'. In yet another Tweet, Trump reconfirmed that the threat from
Soleimani was 'imminent', but in the end it didn't 'really matter because
of his horrible past!'[16] Later on Trump would tell reporters that 'If
Americans anywhere are threatened, we have all of those targets already
fully identified, and I am ready and prepared to take whatever action is
necessary. And that, in particular, refers to Iran.'[17]

So far no one has been charged for the killings. The Iraqi government
called them a 'brazen violation of Iraq's sovereignty', an Iraqi court
issued an arrest warrant for Trump and a report by the UN's special
rapporteur on extrajudicial killings thought it 'unlawful'.[18] Yet the
question of legality missed the point that the US military establishment
heavily invested in developing drones because they offer remote combat
capabilities with the added advantage of plausible deniability. In this
way, drones and other automated, remote weapons systems effectively
bypassed the main statutes of international law that were written for

[15] '"Four Embassies": The Anatomy of Trump's Unfounded Claim about Iran', *The Washington Post*, 13 January 2020. Available at <https://www.washingtonpost.com/politics/four-embassies-the-anatomy-of-trumps-unfounded-claim-about-iran/2020/01/13/2dcd6df0-3620-11ea-bf30-ad313e4ec754_story.html>.
[16] 'How Trump's 'Imminent Threat' on Iran Turned in to the New WMD', *Rolling Stone*, 14 January 2020. Available at <https://www.rollingstone.com/politics/politics-news/imminent-threat-turned-weapons-mass-destruction-937039/>.
[17] 'US Has All Targets Identified if Americans Are Threatened – Trump', *Tass*, 3 January 2020. Available at <https://tass.com/world/1105581>.
[18] 'Soleimani Attack: What Does International Law Say?', *BBC News*, 7 January 2020. Available at <https://www.bbc.com/news/world-51007961>; 'Qasem Soleimani: US Strike on Iran General Was Unlawful, UN Expert Says', *BBC News*, 9 July 2020. Available at <https://www.bbc.com/news/world-middle-east-53345885>, and 'Iraqi Court Orders Trump Arrest over Soleimani Drone Strike', *Al Jazeera*, 7 January 2021. Available at <https://www.aljazeera.com/news/2021/1/7/iraq-court-orders-trump-arrest-over-drone-attack-on-iran-general>.

traditional forms of warfare. Soleimani could be killed in a third country without any declaration of war and simply by remote control without any US casualties. This is the democratization of death that drone warfare has brought about. In theory, anyone, anywhere can be a target.[19]

AI Technology exacerbates this problem of accountability, as the killing of Soleimani is not the only example for the way these new technologies are employed to transcend questions of national sovereignty and to democratize death. This became clear when one year after his death, the Israeli intelligence services spearheaded the murder of an Iranian civilian (in front of the eyes of his wife). Mohsen Fakhrizadeh was not the first scientist involved in Iran's nuclear energy programme to be targeted. But it was the first time that an Iranian civilian was killed by a computerized sharpshooter robot equipped with AI technology and multiple-camera eyes, operated remotely via satellite. The Israeli government didn't use a drone as it would have been easily detected and shot down by Iran's air defence systems. So this robotic machine gun, seemingly premised on the Belgian-made FN MAG capable of firing 600 rounds a minute, was specially manufactured to fit in the bed of an Iranian Zamyad pick-up truck that was packed with explosives so it could self-destruct after the killing.[20]

The future of warfare

Speed, efficiency and contracting the space between us and the killing machine under the purview of the state has always been one of the major aims of modern systems of governance. In short, there is truly nowhere to hide anymore as access and accessibility has ceased to be a

---

[19]   See further Grégoire Chamayou, *A Theory of the Drone*, New York: The New Press, 2015.
[20]   For an uncomfortably 'enthusiastic' account of this killing, see 'The Scientist and the A.I.-Assisted, Remote-Control Killing Machine', *The New York Times*, 18 September 2021. Available at <https://www.nytimes.com/2021/09/18/world/middleeast/iran-nuclear-fakhrizadeh-assassination-israel.html>.

problem of geography. We are all made to float on a topography that is undergirded by a matrix that is entirely connected. I have argued that the Enlightenment suspended the sovereignty of the 'other'. Some of the most dominant Western discourses between the eighteenth and the early-twentieth centuries have invariable functioned to legitimate domination. The ontology of our contemporary technosis emerged out of this ideological habitat. It continues to be engineered on the premise that the leading nations, the so-called 'West', have the moral duty to rescue humanity from disaster. The United States, to the envy of many classical imperialists in Europe, emerged as the enforcer of this right to pre-empt in order to 'pacify' and the tech-giants are invariably acting as enablers. You don't hear, for instance, the CEO of the Chinese based video-focused social sharing platform TikTok talking about changing everyone's life and fighting for civilization in the way that the leaders of the US based tech-companies do.

In the hands of the state and in particularly the techno-military complex, this neo-imperial ideology flags war as merely one signpost of a universal mission to engineer a world order that is amenable to the interest of the ruling classes in the United States, not to be conflated with the majority of the people in the country who are innocent bystanders and at times victims, as indicated. As discussed, when Jalal al-e Ahmad deprecated the onslaught of the machine comparing it to a 'cancer', he was also referring to its victims in the West. From the traditional imperialist perspective, the ambition to make the world available for domination was never bound to geographic delimitation and it was always a distinctly anti-human policy, vertically within society and horizontally in the international system. It is just that technology has seriously multiplied the reach of these classes of society, which allows for a constant attack on the sovereignty of the multitudes all over the world.

The problem is, of course, that the new technologies are permeable and that access and accessibility are not easily contained in one direction. The circular logic of the new death techniques has already democratized drone warfare. The more prominent examples at the time of writing are Turkey, which has deployed so called 'kamikaze drones' with biometric facial recognition in various battlefields including in Libya and Iraq, whilst Israel's Harpy loitering munition – which hangs about in the sky looking for an unrecognized radar signal to strike – has been sold to several countries. Likewise, so-called Perdix drones shot out of an F/A-18 Super Hornet could be scaled to tens of thousands of drones, creating a weapon akin to a low-scale nuclear device.[21] Such drones communicate with one another using a distributed brain complex formation, travelling across a battlefield, and re-forming into a new formation. Iran, too, has a burgeoning drone industry and has exported the technology to allies in Venezuela, Lebanon, Yemen, Iraq, Palestine and elsewhere. So the more sinister impact of AI-driven technology will be on the battlefield, in that realm of human activity where questions of life and death are determined by a split-second decision.

Already, civilians are routinely killed by military drones piloted by humans. In the future we will face a mode of warfare that compounds the problem of killing without accountability. It is not only that killer drones could easily fall into the hands of terrorists. But such AI-driven 'terror-bots' open up immensely challenging questions about ethics on the battlefield. Our current legal system, certainly the Geneva Convention, seem woefully outdated to deal with an army of machines that are programmed to kill, a dystopian future that the former CEO of Google parent company Alphabet, Eric Schmidt, pondered in a detailed report as the head of the US National Security Commission on Artificial Intelligence.[22]

The report concluded that the United States should not agree to ban the use or development of autonomous weapons powered by AI software. It was couched in the language that I have identified as a

---

[21] Zachary Kallenborn, 'Meet the Future Weapon of Mass Destruction, the Drone Swarm', *Bulletin of the Atomic Scientist*, 5 April 2021. Available at <https://thebulletin. org/2021/04/meet-the-future-weapon-of-mass-destruction-the-drone-swarm>.

[22] 'Final Report: National Security Commission on Artificial Intelligence', *National Security Commission on Artificial Intelligence*, March 2021. Available at <https://www. nscai.gov/2021-final-report/>.

legacy of the Enlightenment, with that emphasis on universalizing values, the civilizational mission to engage the world from the position of an imposed moral superiority. Unsurprisingly, for the authors of the report, the global AI competition is also a battle for values between democracies and authoritarian systems such as Russia and China. The 15 members of the commission should know. They included the current CEO of Amazon Andrew Jassy, the Chief Scientific Officer of Microsoft Eric Horvitz, the CEO of the technology company Oracle and Google Cloud AI Director Andrew Moore. All of them agreed, that the US 'will not be able to defend against AI-enabled threats without ubiquitous AI capabilities and new warfighting paradigms.'[23]

Tech-emancipation

There is no suggestion here or any other part of the book that technology is singularly destructive. The topic of the book revolves around the problems with AI and the historical context feeding into our current 'malware' systems. Therefore I have been looking at the nefarious impacts of AI technology in particular. Indeed, even in warfare, AI technology can also prove to be supportive to forms of resistance against an invasion. In the case of the Russian assault on Ukraine in February 2022, for instance, a citizen-like app with a feature called E-Enemy was launched on the platform Diia and administered by the Ukrainian Ministry of Digital Transformation. Diia required users to login through detailed authentication via e-passports in order to avert Russian bots swamping the system with disinformation. Once users logged into E-Enemy via Diia, they were transferred to a Telegram chatbot that asked them about basic information about the nature of the Russian troops, if they are infantry or include vehicles, their size and the time of the sighting or the nature of contact. According to the

---

[23]   Ibid., p. 2.

Ministry of Digital Information in Ukraine, over 260,000 people have used the app in the first weeks of the war.[24]

Furthermore there is a growing counter-narrative to the effort to embed AI technology in a neo-imperial discourse about a seemingly eternal battle between us and them. In 2015, at the International Joint Conference on Artificial Intelligence in Buenos Aires, thousands of concerned AI computer scientists, robotic researchers, professors such as the late Stephen Hawking, Noam Chomsky and even industry leaders such as Elon Musk and Jack Dorsey presented an open letter which called for a ban on autonomous weapons that could be deployed for offensive wars: 'AI technology has reached a point where the deployment of such systems is – practically if not legally – feasible within years, not decades, and the stakes are high: autonomous weapons have been described as the third revolution in warfare, after gunpowder and nuclear arms'.[25] This view was echoed by the House of Lords in the United Kingdom, which urged that the 'prejudices of the past must not be unwittingly built into automated systems, and such systems must be carefully designed from the beginning'.[26] In 2019, a major conference organized by UNESCO in São Paulo calibrated a response from Latin America and the Caribbean calling for a humanistic approach to AI technology and its usage.[27]

Based on these beginnings of an institutionalized global response to the dangers that we are currently facing without much legal respite, a

---

[24] 'A Citizen-like Chatbot Allows Ukrainians to Report to the Government When They Spot Russian Troops – Here's How It Works', *Insider*, 18 April 2022. Available at <https://www.businessinsider.com/ukraine-military-e-enemy-telegram-app-2022-4>.

[25] 'Autonomous Weapons: An Open Letter from AI & Robotics Researchers', *Future of Life Institute*, 28 July 2015. Available at <https://futureoflife.org/2016/02/09/open-letter-autonomous-weapons-ai-robotics/>.

[26] 'AI in the UK: Ready, Willing and Able? – Government Response to the Select Committee Report', *UK House of Lords*, Report of session 2017-19, 16 April 2017, p. 5. Available at <https://publications.parliament.uk/pa/ld201719/ldselect/ldai/100/100.pdf>.

[27] 'UNESCO Promotes a Human-rights Based Approach to AI Development during the Regional Forum on AI in Latin America and the Caribbean', *UNESCO*, 21 April 2022. Available at <https://www.unesco.org/en/articles/unesco-promotes-human-rights-based-approach-ai-development-during-regional-forum-ai-latin>.

decolonial agenda to the development of military AI-systems acknowledges that lethal AI will seriously disrupt the existing United Nations charter and its legal under-belly, which have been built around questions of human security. We urgently need global norms of appropriate behaviour that outlaws the offensive use of AI weapons systems much in the same way as the Chemical Weapons Convention does. To that end, a new discourse has to emerge that is curated around established forms of cultural diplomacy, shifting the language away from divisive 'us-versus-them' paradigms such as the clash of civilization or a new war between 'Western democracies' and 'authoritarian regimes' in China, Russia or Iran.

The necessity to create a creolized AI-discourse imbued with multicultural stamina is possible and necessary, because the proliferation of lethal AI weapons systems increases the likelihood of war. As we have established in this chapter: Drone warfare is already diminishing the ceiling for targeted killings to happen. A decolonial agenda is not merely about cleansing our historical archives from the crimes of the past. But exactly a strategy to create a humanistic scaffolding around AI systems that is strong enough to carry the weight of our existential challenges. Decolonizing Artificial Intelligence must start by genetically modifying the rhizome of knowledge as it has grown in the bewildering jungle of the Social Sciences and the Humanities. To explain exactly what I mean by this last sentence will be the task of the following conclusion to this book.

Decolonized AI: A Manifesto for the Future

In this book my interest in AI was driven by a suspicion that this technological revolution harbours several dangers for humankind, if we don't supervise its usage. In our techno-society every email that we send, online store that we visit, WhatsApp message that we open is monitored and traced. The interfaces between us and AI technologies seem endless. For another example: At some of the latest tech-fairs that I visited, various companies advertised Wi-Fi diapers that would tell you when to change your toddler. In such an environment 'anonymity' is not merely a virtue, it is a scarce resource. Certainly, the world-wide news that a programme called Pegasus, the spyware manufactured by Israel's NSO Group, has been used to track and trace academics, journalists and activists all over the world, must have shattered the myth that common people are not victims of such weapons of mass surveillance. Once spyware such as Pegasus infiltrates your phone it can harvest any data from your device, including from your WhatsApp, photos, SMS messages, etc. It can even switch on your microphone and listen to your conversations and track your every move via your phone's GPS system.

No one seems to be safe. Even so-called privacy browsers that are meant to make it impossible that we are tracked don't seem to help. In May 2022, it was revealed that the DuckDuckGo privacy browser for Android and IDevice Operating System (iOS – Apple) phones didn't do what it promises: constraining the ability of third parties to track users, in particular by blocking tracker cookies, in this case from

Microsoft.[1] Such attacks on our privacy explain why the 'Hacktivist' group Anonymous chose their name, as they emerge out of the labyrinthine ethers of the world-wide-web. Their name serves as a reminder that our privacy is a coveted resource not to be traded. The right to be anonymous needs to be defended in this age of X-ray accessibility to our private lives.

Recent scholarship has established that various forms of so-called 'Hacktivism' have emerged as a cyborg-resistance strategy. As I have argued in Chapter 1, the cyborg challenges our cosy binaries as he/she fuses the fundamental human–robot dichotomy into a new transhuman configuration that is devoid of strict categorization.[2] And yet the battle against the intrusions and trade of our privacy is proving to be difficult. In the most recent example, the data brokerage firm LexisNexis, better known as a search engine for scholarly and legal research, signed a US$16.8 million contract to sell users' information on their database to US Immigration and Customs Enforcement.[3] What I have called digital imperialism is an ever-increasing threat to our human security, as it is turning our everyday existence into a commodity easily traded among self-interested tech-firms and their enablers.

In addition, I have argued that in the future, international power will not be calculated in terms of the strength of traditional military hardware, but the destructive force of algorithms. China calls this 'intelligentized warfare' in its latest five-year plan. International theorists, from the ancient Chinese philosopher Sun Tzu to the former US Secretary of State Henry Kissinger, measured power in terms of materiality. Yet, Sun Tzu, who lived through the tumultuous era covering the area of contemporary China in the sixth century BCE, was famous

---

[1] 'DuckDuckGo Privacy Browser App Does Not Block Microsoft Trackers', *Ghacks*, 25 May 2022. Available at <https://www.ghacks.net/2022/05/25/duckduckgo-privacy-browser-app-does-not-block-microsoft-trackers/>.

[2] For an interesting foray into this see Hans Asenbaum, 'Cyborg Activism: Exploring the Reconfigurations of Democratic Subjectivity in Anonymous', *New Media and Society*, 20, No. 4 (2018), 1543–1563.

[3] 'LexisNexis to Provide Giant Database of Personal Information to ICE', *The Intercept*, 2 April 2021. Available at <https://theintercept.com/2021/04/02/ice-database-surveillance-lexisnexis/>.

for his dictum about how to win a war without having to battle. This was not about 'soft power'. Sun Tzu pioneered a sophisticated psychological war strategy that the Generals of the People's Liberation Army (PLA) in contemporary China term 'cognitive warfare'. This is a new battlefield where our minds are targeted by AI technology as a part of a wider competition for global suzerainty.

Leading strategists in China do not limit war to material factors such as military capability. As a matter of fact, they pay more attention to the cognitive domain, that is psychological strategies that would affect the emotions, motives, judgements and feelings of the enemy. Senior current and former functionaries of the PLA such as Guo Yunfei, President of the Information Engineering University of the PLA's Strategic Support Forces, are busy developing AI technologies that target the brain, for instance through electromagnetic means.[4] Undoubtedly, we have already entered the realm of virtual, mnemonic power that transposes our Alexas and Siris into a borderless canvas inscribed into forms of hybrid warfare. Technology has always been the advantage of empires as speed and pursuit are at the heart of all conquest. But this imperialism is penetrative on an entirely different scale.

Therefore, there is a new world order emerging that transposes the great game of global domination increasingly into the murky ethers of the virtual world and its supersonic AI-induced identities. The Russian invasion of Ukraine in February 2022 is a case in point. US-based tech companies such as Google, Apple, Intel or Meta were quick to cut off supplies and suspend services to Russia. Official accounts tied to the Russian state were mostly 'restricted' by Twitter, Facebook, YouTube, Instagram etc. In response, Russia galvanized its own 'national internet' called RUNET. These cyberwars are determining factors of world politics and this book tried to show how and why.

---

[4]   See further Koichiro Takagi, 'The Future of China's Cognitive Warfare: Lessons from the War in Ukraine', *War on the Rocks*, 22 July 2022. Available at <https://warontherocks. com/2022/07/the-future-of-chinas-cognitive-warfare-lessons-from-the-war-in-ukraine/>.

The new sub-field of 'digital authoritarianism' speaks to some of these concerns.[5] For example, in 2018 an Egyptian Court condemned Amal Fathy to a two-year prison sentence because she had posted a Facebook video about her experiences with sexual harassment in Egypt. Valuable research by the European Council for Foreign Relations has unearthed evidence about the cybercampaigns of the Israeli state and its negative effects on news coverage and human security in Palestine. For instance in 2021, Facebook (Meta) conceded that it made mistakes in removing content about the forced evictions of Palestinians from their homes in the Sheikh Jarrah district of Jerusalem.[6] Surveillance capitalism merges with digital authoritarianism here, as many Israeli tech-firms recruit from governmental intelligence agencies such as Unit 8200 that specializes in surveillance techniques. As the Deputy Commander of Unit 8200 recently conceded during the 2022 Cyber Week at Tel Aviv University: 'We are privileged to have a huge amount of talent, as each year we recruit over 1,000 of the brightest girls and boys in Israel as they join the IDF at the age of 18. This also makes our personnel very young. Over 70% are under the age of 23.'[7]

It does not come as a surprise to those scholars who have studied the administrative web cast over Palestine by the Israeli state, that such start-up firms are heavily implicated in surveillance techniques, in this case in a wide-ranging facial recognition network across the West Bank. This surveillance regime is so obviously oppressive, whilst technically opaque, that it triggered a protest letter by 34 Israeli reserve soldiers who had served in Unit 8200: 'We, veterans of Unit 8200 . . . declare that we refuse to take part in actions against Palestinians and refuse to

---

[5]   See further Marc Owen Jones, *Digital Authoritarianism in the Middle East: Deception, Disinformation and Social Media*, London: Hurst, 2022, or Babak Rahimi and David Farid (eds.), *Social Media in Iran: Politics and Society after 2009*, New York: State University of New York Press, 2015.

[6]   See James Lynch, 'Iron Net: Digital Repression in the Middle East and North Africa', *European Council on Foreign Relations*, 29 June 2022. Available at <https://ecfr.eu/publication/iron-net-digital-repression-in-the-middle-east-and-north-africa/>.

[7]   'Deputy Commander of Elite Intelligence Unit 8200 Reveals Its Secret Weapon', *Israel Forbes*, 30 June 2022. Available at <https://forbes.co.il/e/deputy-commander-of-elite-intelligence-unit-8200-reveals-its-secret-weapon/>.

continue serving as tools in deepening the military control over the Occupied Territories.[8] In 2021, the Israeli company at the heart of the face recognition project, AnyVision, secured US$235 million in further investments from the Japan-based SoftBank group, which in turn has been backed by Saudi Arabia's Public Investment Fund.[9] The motto of the SoftBank group is: 'Information Revolution – Happiness for everyone'.[10] This is a very neat example for the nexus between surveillance capitalism, digital authoritarianism and the 'go-happy' lifestyle narrative that is so central to the internationalized Silicon Valley culture.

While the book has been primarily about explaining the dangers of some of these inventions and global trends for human security, I have also tried to maintain that technology can function as an instrument of resistance as even the most sophisticated algorithm can be defused. This is largely steeped in my conceptual and theoretical persuasion and previous research, which implicates power and resistance inside each other.[11] Where there is power, there will always be resistance. But it is also due to the empirical fact that technology is permeable, which implies that it can be used in any direction: To discipline and punish and/or to emancipate and liberate. For every 'SS-bot' that magnifies learned biases and turns them into a form of neural fascism, we can have a counter-mnemonic that churns out socially just algorithms that encode equality.

For example, when the tech-company Quilt.AI teamed up with the Singapore-based gender-awareness advocacy organization AWAKE, they produced a valuable study into online misogyny in Singapore. The machine-learning model developed by Quilt.AI demonstrated that

---

8   'Israeli Intelligence Veterans' Letter to Netanyahu and Military Chiefs – in Full'. *The Guardian*, 12 September 2014. <https://www.theguardian.com/world/2014/sep/12/israeli-intelligence-veterans-letter-netanyahu-military-chiefs>.

9   'Lynch, 'Iron Net: Digital Repression in the Middle East and North Africa'.

10 See <https://group.softbank/en>.

11 See further Arshin Adib-Moghaddam, *On the Arab Revolts and the Iranian Revolution: Power and Resistance Today*, London: Bloomsbury, 2006, or Adib-Moghaddam, 'Can the (Sub)altern Resist?: A Dialogue between Foucault and Said', in Ian Richard Netton, (ed.), *Orientalism Revisited: Art, Land, Voyage*. Abingdon: Routledge, 2012.

female accounts on Twitter received 'twice as many misogynistic comments as a random sample of accounts. In terms of engagement, misogynistic comments were twice as likely to be "liked" and 4.5 times more likely to be retweeted when compared to non-misogynistic comments.'[12]

Another commendable project led by Quilt.AI and the International Center for Research on Women revealed that during the Covid crisis online harassment of women in various cities and rural areas in India, namely Assagao, Kangra, Palakkad, and Gaya, on the one side and Bengaluru, Delhi, Mumbai, and Kolkata on the other, increased manifold.[13] At Goldsmiths, University of London, Eyal Weizman is heading the 'Forensic Architecture' team, which surveys human rights abuses all over the world by using architectural technologies. Even in authoritarian political settings such as in Iran, conferences about Ophthalmology and other specialized fields that are essentially non-political, are used to delve deeper into the social repercussions of AI technology and their implications for society. Some of the methodologies espoused may seem improvable from the perspective of a critical social scientist, but such efforts are very good examples about some of the productive movements that the AI world opens up. Once these are merged into a wider strategy geared to decolonial emancipation, they become valuable sites to address our political and social challenges.

Digital power – human resistance

Even if algorithms rule the world, we can poison them if they are unjust. Indeed, people all over the world are routinely engaged in 'data strikes',

---

[12] Thanks to Quilt.AI's Angad Chowdhry for pointing me to this study. See 'Online Misogyny Manifests in Resentment around National Service and Misconceptions around Gender-based Violence, and Sees High Engagement: Quilt.AI and AWARE study', TFSV, 2 September 2021. Available at <https://www.aware.org.sg/2021/09/online-misogyny-quilt-ai-aware-study/>.

[13] See further Quilt.AI and the International Centre for Research on Women, 'Online Violence in the Time of COVID-19', 16 April 2021. Available at <https://www.quilt.ai/post/online-violence-during-covid-19>.

concerted efforts to withhold or delete their data so that tech firms can't access them or to contribute harmful/meaningless data that can't be used to personalize advertisement – a US$ 120 billion business for companies such as Google. Research in this direction needs to be furthered by zooming into forms of resistance against technological oppression. For instance, the Iranian state may administer some of the most stringent internet rules. But a new Android App developed by tech-savvy Iranian entrepreneurs encrypts up to 1,000 characters of Persian text into an undecipherable jumble of words. You can send this mélange to a friend over any communication platform – Telegram, WhatsApp, Google Chat, etc. – and then they run it through the App on their device to decipher what you've said in order to get around any censorship administered by the state through their track-and-trace software.

These are forms of techno-resistance happening right now. They are a potent field of research and disruptive social practice for the new generation of critical philosophers/social scientists. In some Eastern thought-systems, certainly in Muslim philosophy, the 'veil' was never merely about covering the female body, but also about ensuring one's anonymity and privacy and shielding it from nefarious forces. The current waves of 'data strikes' that are also advocated by Hacktivist groups such as Anonymous, are a form of data veiling – a powerful shield from the penetrative QR code that scans our everyday lives and which is branded upon our bodies by the so-called tech-giants. I would recommend to be a pious 'online Muslim' or a 'cyber-Nun' in that regard – digital veiling in opposition to digital oppression.

At the heart of the ethics of AI, I have placed the search for perfection. Enlightenment thought in Europe tried to establish what Nietzsche so aptly called the 'Übermensch'. I have argued that the myth of racial superiority – that Nietzsche isn't to blame for – was codified, theorized and taught via several dangerous cob-sciences that professed racial superiority and promised to scientifically prove the domination of the 'Aryan man' as a necessary progression of human kind. In this process of extremist social Darwinism all the 'creole' subject peoples would be erased in favour of the pure master race. White Supremacists still believe in this nonsense. Thanks to decades of research, and certainly galvanized by Edward Said's 'Orientalism', we know by now that this pseudo-scientific racism undergirded both the imperial enterprise of Europe, that is the domination of 'subject races' as a civilizational project, and more seriously Nazi ideology which led to the horrors of the Holocaust.[14]

In the present book I have studied the normative attitude underlying AI research, as a part of this trajectory of Western Enlightenment thought and its search for perfection, as artificial intelligence transposes this quest for the ultimate 'master race' from the human to the machine. This anti-human perfectionism is already impacting the labour market, where AI technology is the next step in the Fordist premise of maximum productivity. My argument developed this philosophy of AI, not so much as a Doomsday manual, but a genuine attempt to embed this new dawn of technological revolution in a wider discussion about its consequences for society. As a part of my method, I opened up patterns in Global Thought, from the suspicion towards the 'machine' in the writings of the Iranian intellectual of the 1960s, Jalal al-e Ahmad, the 'coloniality of power' conceptualised by the Peruvian thinker Aníbal Quijano to the dialectic of the Enlightenment of Theodor Adorno and Max Horkheimer, the doyens of the 'Frankfurt School' in Germany.

I have shown how advances in AI research are already determining the new world order. This is why China has premised all of its development strategies on advances in AI. It is projected in several very recent research papers that within a decade automation will replace half of the current jobs.[15] So at least in this transition to a new digitized, e-economy, many people will lose their livelihoods. Even if we assume that this so-called 'Fourth Industrial Revolution' will level itself up, and a new workforce will emerge entirely well versed to navigate and command this data-dominated world, we would still have to face major

---

[14]   Edward Said, *Orientalism*, London: Vintage, 1979.
[15]   'Machines to "do half of all work tasks by 2025"', *BBC News*, 21 October 2020. Available at <https://www.bbc.com/news/business-54622189>.

socio-economic problems in this transition phase. The disruptions will be immense and need to be scrutinized especially in the Global South and among the poorer strata of society all over the world, certainly also in Europe and North America.

The ultimate aim of AI, even narrow AI, is to perfect every cognitive task that a human being can manage. Eventually, machine-learning systems may well be programmed to be better at everything without, of course, the human touch, empathy, love, hate or any other self-conscious emotion that make us human. In the perfectly productive world – exactly that world that both the racists and the hyper-capitalists of the Enlightenment period imagined – humankind would be a burden. We would be accounted as worthless, certainly in terms of productivity, but also in terms of our feeble humanity. AI systems are programmed to be better than humans at every task that we are doing. So unless we substitute an economistic attitude towards life that positions productivity and 'material growth' above sustainability and individual happiness, AI research will be another chain in the history of self-defeating human inventions.

Already we are witnessing racial biases in algorithmic calculations and automated weapons programmed to kill, which are carrying maxims such as 'productivity' and 'efficiency' into the battle-zones of this world, as demonstrated in the previous chapters. As a result, war has become more sustainable as the perpetrators don't have to account for the loss of human lives, which always also carries social resistance. There are less body-bags both to mourn and to galvanize traditional anti-war strategies, which seem increasingly outdated, now. As we have established in the previous chapter, proliferation of drone warfare is a very vivid indicator of these new forms of e-warfare. They create a virtual reality that is almost absent from our consciousness and a global, space-less warzone that is at the same time post-human and post-visual as it happens beyond our TV screens and social media accounts. In this world, peace is really just war by other means. The late Paul Virilio was right about that.

Everything I have said should not validate the rather comical depiction of AI as an inevitable nightmare where we will face an army of super-intelligent 'Terminators' bound to erase the human race. Such dystopian predictions are too crude to capture the nitty gritty of AI, and its impact on our everyday existence. So societies are set to benefit from AI, if they integrate its usage into a wider discussion about the merits in terms of sustainable economic development and human security. The confluence of power and AI, for instance investment into systems of control and surveillance, should not substitute for the promise of a humanized AI, that puts technology in the service of the individual, and not the other way around. The obsession with perfection and 'hyper-efficiency' has had a profound impact on human relations, even human reproduction as people live their lives in cloistered, virtual realities of their own making. For instance, several US- and China-based companies have produced robotic dolls that are selling out fast as substitute wives. One man in China even married his cyber-doll. A woman in France married a robo-man advertising her love story as a form of 'robo-sexuality' and campaigning to legalize her marriage. The very existence of the human race is therefore challenged from various directions: hyper-warfare, environmental degradation and/or robotic wives and husbands that also function as compliant sexual objects, the former obviously without any chance of reproduction.[16]

One thing that I am very positive about is the inability of AI to substitute philosophy, intellectuality and the human touch. To be a real philosopher, after all requires empathy, having a heart. If we can programme our machines to consider this, then AI research has the capacity to improve our lives, which should be the ultimate aim of any technological advance. If AI research yields a new ideology centred around the notion of perfectionism and maximal productivity, then it will be a destructive force, that will lead to more wars, more famines and more social and economic distress, especially for the poor. At this juncture of global history, this choice is still ours.

---

[16]   See further Isabell Millar, *The Psychoanalysis of Artificial Intelligence*, London: Palgrave, 2021.

GoodThink Inc

In his oft-cited ending to the *Order of Things*, an exploration of the Western human sciences, Michel Foucault famously stipulated that man might be simply 'erased, like a face drawn in sand at the edge of the sea'.[17] Foucault spoke of a specific Enlightenment creature, Western man, that subdued everyone that he considered different: women, homosexuals, other cultures and peoples. The Covid-19 pandemic out of which this book emerged intellectually made it abundantly clear that 'Mensch' wants to survive and that she is quite capable to do so. What is needed to that end is a positive, life-affirming appreciation that emancipation and real freedom from any form of oppression is continuously possible. Our algorithms need to be charged with a language of poetic empathy, love, hope and care, in order to churn out just calculations.

This GoodThink that I am advocating gains sustenance from various directions. The 'extinction rebellion' and the new environmental romanticists forging multilateral cooperation against and around the threat of global warming or space-unbound influenzas caused by post-penicillin viruses such as H1N1 ('Swine Flu') or H5N1 ('Bird Flu') and Covid-19 (see below), are very good and current examples for the possibility of the task. They are promising not only because of the citizen-led global forms of solidarity that they have already engendered. But also because some specific research, for instance into deoxyribonucleic acid (DNA), marks a scientific departure from racial and anatomical hierarchies that were central to the cob-sciences of the phrenologists of the nineteenth century, the eugenic experiments of the Nazis, the haematologists of the mid-twentieth century and the ideologies of contemporary, neo-fascist movements in Europe and North America.[18]

---

[17] Michel Foucault, *The Order of Things: An Archaeology of the Human Sciences*, London: Vintage, 1973, p. 387.
[18] See T.A. Jones, 'The Restoration Gene Pool Concept: Beyond the Native Versus Non-native Debate', *Restoration Ecology*, 11, No. 3, 2003, 281–290.

Furthermore, the structure of DNA – *The Double Helix* invented discovered by James D. Watson and Francis Crick, and the Human Genome Project launched by the US Congress with an initial federal budget of US$3 billion in 1988 – does not only point to our atomized biological constitution. It also implies that we are all made of the same stuff. If you and I are constituted of the same chemical formulas, we may be able to mitigate some of our differences on that basis. Once our common humanity is realized, the current transhuman trends into incorporating a cyborg identity into our human consciousness ceases to be an act of bodily violation. Instead it turns into a life-affirming opportunity for synthesis and integration.

Writers such as Shirlee Taylor Haizlip in her autobiographical memoir *The Sweeter the Juice* engage with this ameliorating future that the de-codification of the genome promises. To Haizlip, such research shows that race is a social construction rather than a genetic reality. This is true. But at the same time DNA research also entails all the ingredients of a potentially dangerous dystopia. Behind it lurks one of the most central legacies of the Enlightenment project that I have discussed in this book: The fascination with perfection, the current obsession with the perfect body image being a related pathology. However paranoid the vision of a genetically 'purified' world, we are right to fear it when every news bulletin brings breaking research on how foetuses can be altered in the womb and genes in plants, animals and perhaps human beings can be manipulated, whether for profit or prophylaxis. Disability rights activists alert us to something real when they insist that we suffer an immeasurable loss when we value life only in terms of its functionality and flawlessness.[19]

When it comes to moving to a critical appreciation of the way the natural sciences can contribute to a new understanding of self and other, one has to start where al-e Ahmad, Marcuse and the theorists of the Frankfurt School left: with criticism of the ways the human species

---

[19]   Sarah E. Chinn, *Technology and the Logic of American Racism: A Cultural History of the Body as Evidence*, London: Continuum, 2000, p. 168.

has contributed to the destruction of the natural habitat, with a critical analysis of the ways the science of nature has contributed to the oppression of its subject. This calls for nothing short of a re-enchantment with nature, a dialectical communication between the individual and her natural habitat in which the latter acknowledges the uncontrollable trans-spatiality of the former. So construed, as a realm of interdependent particularity, nature, the earth becomes a source of resistance to the divisive tendencies that are so central to the anthropocentric notions adopted from the perspective of Western modernity. Contemporary critical theorists put it this way: the pseudo-objective 'science' informed by an interest in control and exploitation would have to give away 'to a "metascience" whose full normative context includes reference to ethics, values, social justice, and ecology'.[20] Real-life examples of this GoodThink are not as far away as one may think. In fact, they were readily observable during the most devastating crisis of my generation: The horrific Covid-19 pandemic.

Pandemic connectivity

In the middle of the coronavirus pandemic, I wrote an article for *The Conversation*, that elicited several responses that speak to the decolonial manifesto and the GoodThink that I am trying to charter. The article was entitled 'Bani Adam' and referred to a form of 'coronavirus solidarity' and how a thirteenth-century mystical Persian poem about humanity demonstrates why we need a global response to global challenges such as Covid-19, or AI for that matter. The last sentence of the article summarizes the crux of my message: 'It's time that we act upon the science, with the empathy of a poet, and institute a new form of internationalism'.[21]

---

[20] Steven Best and Douglas Kellner, *The Postmodern Turn*, London: The Guildford Press, 1997, p. 269.

[21] Arshin Adib-Moghaddam, 'Bani Adam: The 13th-century Persian Poem That Shows Why Humanity Needs a Global Response to Coronavirus', *The Conversation*, 27 March 2020. Available at <https://theconversation.com/bani-adam-the-13th-century-persian-poem-that-shows-why-humanity-needs-a-global-response-to-coronavirus-134836>.

The short piece was written at a time of serious distress and anxiety for many people, and it was meant to make a point about human connectivity during a period of profound loneliness, buttressed by lockdowns, social distancing and quarantines. The responses to the article, in particular on the *Yahoo News* webpage and *The Dawn* website of India that republished it among dozens of other outlets, motivated me to delve deeper into notions of identity, and to connect to my previous research, in particular because of the rather more aggressive comments, that reminded me about the artificial formations of 'identity' that are weaved into our daily existence as consumers of politics and the (social) media.

The article, as much as this book, was all about how human solidarity can overcome challenges to human security. GoodThink refers to our common bonds that are densely interwoven into a global human fabric. It is meant to bring people together even at that time when we had to live apart, banned to our homes, policed to stay there or thereabouts, without much recourse to society. My own situation was emblematic. Cooped up in my study, I was worried about my 85-year-old father who was stranded in Tehran, my sister, a doctor and pharmacologist in Hamburg, and my elderly mother who had to self-isolate in order to prevent contracting Covid-19, due to her underlying medical conditions. Like everyone else, I was horrified about the rising numbers of deaths all over the world and especially in Europe and the United States. So philosophy became a remedy and analytical tool to understand and cope with a catastrophic situation and a seemingly dark future, as the 'new normal' of self-isolation had to be accepted as such.

But my ambition was not merely normative, or driven by some kind of intellectual survival instinct. The article (and its discontent) became a part of a serious effort to reveal as false, the grand notions of identity, for instance the 'West' and 'Islam', as I have been repeatedly attacked by people, who hide behind the artificial mask of both. It is factual, that this variant of SARS-CoV-2 reaffirmed that humanity is bound by a common fate that highlights connections, mutuality, interdependence and hybridity, and not only in cultural terms, but exactly in terms of our biological constitution as *homo sapiens*. Covid-19 doesn't care about Islam and the West, China or Japan. It must have been quite clear to everyone, that our differences are superficial.

Pandemics like Covid-19 demonstrate that discrimination on the basis of race, gender, religion, sexual orientation or else are self-defeating, because there is a little bit of us in every other human being. This is the GoodThink attitude that needs to feed into our algorithms, too, as I have argued in this book from a similar ontological perspective. Why else were we asked to self-isolate? It was not only to protect ourselves, but to safeguard society, the 'other', who had to be artificially distanced from us exactly because of our inevitable intimacy. In this specific sense, the virus demonstrated an eerie egalitarianism. It was non-discriminatory, as it could be contracted by anyone. You could be the most 'pious' Christian evangelical or Islamist, but the virus would act upon your body much in the same way as it would on the most ardent atheist. I saw Ayatollah Khomeini, Richard Dawkins and Bill Graham all in the same boat, at least from this anthropomorphic, medico-philosophical perspective.

Covid-19 must have made it abundantly clear, literally with virulent pace, that such pandemics defy geography, and merge spaces. The epidemic curve of the virus could only shoot up with such frightening speed, because of our globalitarian trans-localities. We are all local and tied to an all-encompassing humanity at the same time. This transactional connectivity between our bodies, which was reflected in the exponential growth of infections on a global scale, prompted the World Health Organisation (WHO) to declare Covid-19 a pandemic, defined as the worldwide spread of a new disease, at quite an early stage after the virus was first detected in Wuhan, in the Hubei province of China, a largely landlocked area. This categorization of Covid-19 as a global pandemic, came as early as the 11 March 2020, when the number of cases outside of China, 'increased 13-fold and the number of affected countries [had] tripled'.[22] Within this very short period of time, the disease spread from Wuhan, to 114 countries. When I wrote my humble article, two weeks had passed from the WHO declaration, and over 100,000 had been infected. Quite clearly, then, there was no escaping the coronavirus, exactly because humanity is inevitably interdependent. Ayatollah Khomeini, Richard Dawkins and Bill Graham – their biological constitution is the same.

We don't only share such global challenges with our neighbours on the street, but literally with every body all over the world. The incredibly uplifting, self-made videos showing neighbourhoods reaching out to each other by singing, playing music or other forms of social communication are very good examples for the spirit of GoodThink I am alluding to. On the more tragic side, the lockdowns exacerbated existing mental-health problems, anxieties, depression, exactly because we are social animals who need society to exist beyond mere survival. The virtual world was no substitute to the human touch. Zuckerberg is wrong to assume that it ever can be. Even those nasty pictures of panic-buying did not dent the overwhelmingly humane manifestations of solidarity. Consumerism and rampant capitalism may have aided and abetted what the Oxford Professor Richard Dawkins so sinisterly called 'the selfish gene', but in the end our 'social gene' proved to be stronger, and much closer to our biology than such social Darwinists such as Dawkins appreciate.

Young people delivering food to isolated individuals did not act upon some selfish herd mentality. For once, the whole world understood that our feelings are similar: the loneliness and boredom of self-isolation, even its celebration for the introvert, spoke to emotions that were shared. Geography was meaningless, nation-states were reduced to administrative units rather than entities that could be kept entirely apart from each other for eternity. We were all in the same boat facing similar fears and tragedies, and that was the ironic beauty of the lockdown period.

---

[22] 'WHO Director-General's Opening Remarks at the Media Briefing on COVID-19', *World Health Organisation*, 11 March 2020. Available at <https://www.who.int/dg/speeches/detail/who-director-general-s-opening-remarks-at-the-media-briefing-on-covid-19---11-march-2020>.

Politicking a poetic future

In the meantime, many of us are concerned because we are finding out, tragedy by tragedy, that there is a lack of multilateral cooperation when it comes to global challenges including AI. Our elected leaders are incompetent or helpless, and extremist capitalism has focused much of our resources on profit, rather than on institutions that serve the people. The coronavirus transmuted into such an all-encompassing pandemic for two simple reasons. First, our common biology does not respect any of the mental and physical borders that were created to keep us apart. Second, coronavirus revealed how globalized our contemporary world is. Our lives are so closely interlinked and networked that this outbreak travelled all around the world within weeks. The speed at which the virus spread demonstrates quite clearly the contracted space that we are all living in on earth. Yet, in clear contradiction to what is needed, politicians continue to speak of global challenges in terms of mere national emergencies. This approach compartmentalizes what is conjoined, and contributes to the current crisis, which can only be faced properly with global coordination and within multilateral organizations. But the UN and its auxiliary network is despised by the new breed of psycho-nationalist leaders all around the world. It is these leaders who have stunted our ability to resolve borderless challenges such as AI, pandemics and the environmental destruction of our natural habitat.

Of course, even when it comes to pressing issues such as regulating the dangerous impacts of AI, national policies are a necessary starting point. For instance, in March 2022, China's Internet Information Service Algorithm Recommendation Management Regulations were introduced in order to enable Internet users to decline personalized advertisements, thus minimizing the ability of algorithms to present personalized recommendations by tracking activities on the Internet. At the same time, the Chinese state facilitates the export of AI-driven technologies of surveillance, in particular to Sub-Saharan African countries such as Tanzania, Uganda, Rwanda and Ethiopia, which share an approach to governance that is based on bureaucratic management within settings where privacy laws are weak. This is a very different situation to the wealthiest countries in the Americas, Europe and Asia, where civil society is better equipped to appropriate AI-technologies, even for the purpose of political resistance.[23]

As we have established, track-and-trace technology can be used for nefarious agendas without much accountability, surveillance by the state being one of them. The major tech-companies argue that some of this is inevitable as deep learning depends on mathematical processes that are untraceable, even for the engineers. This is how they defy calls for algorithm regulation, algorithm mechanism audits, and outside technology ethics reviews. In turn it explains the ethics deficiency in the AI industry, as regulation is superseded by the rationale to maximize profits. As one scholar who perused all major ethic guidelines in the industry rightly concluded: 'Currently, AI ethics is failing in many cases. Ethics lacks a reinforcement mechanism. . . . And in cases where ethics is integrated into institutions, it mainly serves as a marketing strategy.[24]

The tech-industry offers solutions with great fanfare. But their history is chequered. In a very prominent and recent example, Facebook's parent company Meta announced a massive new open-access language model inviting researchers, including from the Social Sciences and the Humanities, to amend any flaws in its GPT-3 neural network. GPT-3 stands for Generative Pre-trained Transformer 3. It is a neural network machine-learning system developed by Elon Musk's OpenAI, programmed to use internet data to create any type of text. With its over 175 billion machine learning parameters, GPT-3 is better equipped than any prior model for producing text that is convincing enough to seem like a human could have written it. Meta has giving full

[23] Thanks to Matti Pohjonen for forwarding some of the proceeds of a conference at the University of the Witwatersrand that he was involved in. See 'Between Cyberutopia and Cyberphobia: The Humanities on the African Continent in the Era of Machine Learning', University of the Witwatersrand, 7 March 2019.

[24] Thilo Hagendorff, 'The Ethics of AI Ethics: An Evaluation of Guidelines', *Minds and Machines*, 30, No. 1 (March 2020). Available at <https://link.springer.com/article/10.1007/s11023-020-09517-8>.

access to GPT-3 in May 2022, together with details about how the system was built and trained.[25]

It is difficult not to be sceptical about such highly advertised initiatives that are implemented under the close auspices of tech-companies. In the recent past, when the challenges became too comprehensive, tech-companies were either uncooperative as indicated in the previous chapters, or they forced people out because of their critical stance. One of the more prominent cases was Timnit Gebru, the former AI co-lead of Google. Gebru and her colleagues flagged some of the immense risks of large language models in a research paper published in 2020. It was demonstrated among other points that training large AI models consumes immense amounts of computer processing power, and therefore a lot of electricity. This was pointed out as a major concern for the environment as the energy consumption and therefore carbon emissions and financial costs of AI-models has been skyrocketing. Gebru was one of the few black women at Google Research before she was ousted. In 2016, she had co-founded the non-for-profit organization 'Black in AI', which promotes minority access to the AI-industry.[26]

National and industry-led efforts to integrate ethical guidelines into the AI industry and to ensure minority access, need to be connected to the various bodies of the United Nations, in order to amalgamate with and scaffold other local policies, for instance the EU High-Level Expert Group on Artificial Intelligence, which identified five principles for the trustworthy and ethical development of AI: beneficence, nonmaleficence, autonomy of humans, justice, and explicability.

The EU has been regulating tech-firms more aggressively in recent years, for instance in 2022 with the 'Digital Markets Act'. This is an antitrust legislation which aims to prevent tech-giants such as Google

[25]   Douglas Heaven, 'Meta Has Built a Massive New Language AI – And It's Giving It Away for Free', *MIT Technology Review*, 3 May 2022. Available at <https://www.technologyreview.com/2022/05/03/1051691/meta-ai-large-language-model-gpt3-ethics-huggingface-transparency/>.
[26]   See <https://blackinai.github.io/#/>.

or Meta from abusing their dominant market position to block smaller companies from competing with them, for example by creating so-called 'walled gardens'. Essentially, the walled garden directs our online navigation and rotates it within websites that are dominated by the tech-giants, thus marginalizing smaller competitors. Ever wondered why Google seems to be the only effective search engine? This is one of the technical reasons why: The 'walled garden' prevents others to access Google's data.

In May 2022, the EU introduced the Digital Service Act (DSA). It is meant to force companies such as Google and Meta to supervise illegal content on their platforms more comprehensively, or risk being fined. Very comparable to China's Internet Information Service Algorithm Recommendation Management Regulations, the DSA confines how the tech-giants target us with online ads by inhibiting algorithms that are based on gender, race or religious data gathered from our online identity. Targeting children with such identity-based advertisement would also be prohibited.[27]

Such national and regional policies have to be integrated and legally fortified with UN-based initiatives, for instance by the Group of Governmental Experts of the Convention on Certain Conventional Weapons on emerging technologies in the area of lethal autonomous weapon systems (LAWS), which is comprised of 125 states. This grouping, as well, sets out guiding principles that are informed by shared understandings on definitions and the nature of human intervention with a particular emphasis on ethical requirements to screen the various stages of technology development and deployment to uphold compliance with international law, in particular international humanitarian law geared to questions of human security.[28] Crucial

---

[27] 'EU Agrees on Landmark Law Aimed at Forcing Big Tech Firms to Tackle Illegal content', *CNBC*, 22 April 2022. Available at <https://www.cnbc.com/2022/04/22/digital-services-act-eu-agrees-new-rules-for-tackling-illegal-content.html>.

[28] 'Background on LAWS in the CCW'. *United Nations Office for Disarmament Affairs*. Available at <https://www.un.org/disarmament/the-convention-on-certain-conventional-weapons/background-on-laws-in-the-ccw/>.

beginnings by the United Nations have been made, for instance in November 2021, when the 193 Member States at UNESCO's General Conference adopted the Recommendation on the Ethics of Artificial Intelligence, which has set some important global standards.[29] But this ethical scaffolding needs to be enforced from the bottom-up within communities and in our everyday life. Now is the time to act to that end.

* * *

'No man is an island', wrote the poet John Donne in 1624 echoing what the Persian genius Sa'adi proclaimed in his world-renowned poem Bani Adam (human-kind) in the twelfth century. We are at a pivotal juncture of our existence as *homo sapiens*. We are entirely equipped to embrace these challenges with the beautiful empathy of a poet and the critical acumen of those scientists that celebrate our common humanity; our real-world connections that are not neutered and reduced to a sterile, virtual existence. I-Mensch: Here is to a new form of human-centred politics that is worthy of that poetic future.

[29] For further documents and useful materials, refer to this UNESCO website: 'Ethics of Artificial Intelligence'. Available at <https://www.unesco.org/en/artificial-intelligence/recommendation-ethics#:~:text=UNESCO%20Member%20States%20adopt%20the, setting%20instrument%20on%20the%20subject>.

Select Bibliography

Abrams, Jerold J., 'Pragmatism, Artificial Intelligence, and Posthuman Bioethics: Shusterman, Rorty, Foucault', *Human Studies*, 27 (2004), 241–258.

Adams, Rachel, 'Can Artificial Intelligence Be Decolonised?', *Interdisciplinary Science Reviews*, 46, No. 1–2 (2021), 176–197.

Adib-Moghaddam, Arshin, *On the Arab Revolts and the Iranian Revolution: Power and Resistance Today*, London: Bloomsbury, 2006.

Adib-Moghaddam, Arshin, 'A (Short) History of the Clash of Civilisation', *Cambridge Review of International Affairs*, 21, No. 2 (June 2008), 217–234.

Adib-Moghaddam, Arshin, 'Can the (Sub)altern Resist?: A Dialogue between Foucault and Said', in Ian Richard Netton, (ed.), *Orientalism Revisited: Art, Land, Voyage*, Abingdon: Routledge, 2012, 33–54.

Adib-Moghaddam, Arshin, 'Bani Adam: The 13th-century Persian Poem That Shows Why Humanity Needs a Global Response to Coronavirus', *The Conversation*, 27 March 2020. Available at <https://theconversation.com/bani-adam-the-13th-century-persian-poem-that-shows-why-humanity-needs-a-global-response-to-coronavirus-134836>.

Adib-Moghaddam, Arshin, *What Is Iran? Domestic Politics and International Relations in Five Musical Pieces*, Cambridge: Cambridge University Press, 2021.

Adorno, Theodor W. and Max Horkheimer, *Dialectic of Enlightenment*, John Cumming (trans.), London: Verso, 1997.

al-e Ahmad, Jalal, *Plagued by the West (Gharbzadegi)*, translated from the Persian by Paul Sprachman, New York: Caravan, 1982, p. 31.

'An Interview with Mark Zuckerberg about the Metaverse', *Stratechery*, 28 October 2021. Available at <https://stratechery.com/2021/an-interview-with-mark-zuckerberg-about-the-metaverse/>.

Arendt, Hannah, *The Origins of Totalitarianism*, 2nd edn, Cleveland, OH: World Publishing Co., 1958.

Asenbaum, Hans, 'Cyborg Activism: Exploring the Reconfigurations of Democratic Subjectivity in Anonymous', *New Media and Society*, 20, No. 4 (2018), 1543–1563.

Atkinson, Robert D., 'A U.S. Grand Strategy for the Global Digital Economy', *Information Technology and Innovation Foundation*, 19 January 2021.

Available at <https://itif.org/publications/2021/01/19/us-grand-strategy-global-digital-economy>.

Bartoletti, Rachel Ivana, *An Artificial Revolution: On Power, Politics and AI*, London: The Indigo Press, 2020.

Best, Steven and Douglas Kellner, *The Postmodern Turn*, London: The Guildford Press, 1997.

Black, Deborah L., 'Avicenna on Self-Awareness and Knowing that One Knows', in Shahid Rahman, Tony Street, Hassan Tahiri (eds)., *The Unity of Science in the Arabic Tradition: Science, Logic, Epistemology and their Interactions*, Dordrecht: Springer, 2008, 63–88.

Bodde, Derk, 'Chinese Ideas in the West', *Committee on Asiatic Studies in American Education*. Available at <http://projects.mcah.columbia.edu/nanxuntu/html/state/ideas.pdf>.

Bostrom, Nick, *Superintelligence: Paths, Dangers, Strategies*, Oxford: Oxford University Press, 2016.

Chinn, Sarah E., *Technology and the Logic of American Racism: A Cultural History of the Body as Evidence*, London: Continuum, 2000.

Collins, Eli and Zoubin Ghahramani, 'LaMDA: Our Breakthrough Conversation Technology', *Google*, 18 May 2021. Available at <https://blog.google/technology/ai/lamda/>.

Couldry, Nick and Ulises A. Mejias, 'Data Colonialism: Rethinking Big Data's Relation to the Contemporary Subject', *Television & New Media* 20, No. 4 (2019), 336–349.

Crawford, Kate, *Atlas of AI: The Real Worlds of Artificial Intelligence*, New Haven, CT: Yale University Press, 2021.

Cullinane, Michael Patrick and David Ryan (eds.), *U.S. Foreign Policy and the Other*, Oxford: Berghahn, 2014.

Darwin, Charles, *The Origin of Species*, Ware: Wordsworth, 1998.

Darwin, Charles, 'The Descent of Man, and Selection in Relation to Sex', part 2, Paul H. Barrett and R. B. Freeman (eds), *The Works of Charles Darwin*, Vol. 22, New York: New York University Press, 1989.

Darwin, Francis, *Charles Darwin: His Life Told in an Autobiographical Chapter, and in a Selected Series of His Published Letters*, London: Murray, 1902.

Der Derian, James (ed.), *The Virilio Reader*, Oxford: Blackwell, 1998.

D'Ignazio, Catherine and Lauren F. Klein, *Data Feminism*, Cambridge, MA: The MIT Press, 2020.

Eubanks, Virginia, *Automating Inequality: How High-Tech Tools Profile, Police and Punish the Poor*, London: Macmillan, 2018.

Floyd Jr, Lt Col Garry S., 'Attribution and Operational Art: Implications for *Competing in Time*', *Strategic Studies Quarterly*, 12, No. 2 (2018), p. 17 (17–55).

Foucault, Michel, *The Order of Things: An Archaeology of the Human Sciences*, London: Vintage, 1973.

Foucault, Michel, *Society Must Be Defended: Lectures at the Collège de France*, Mauro Bertani and Alessandro Fontana (eds), David Macey (trans.), London: Penguin, 2004.

Fu, Siyao and Zeng-Guang Hou, 'Learning Race from Face: A Survey', *IEEE Transactions on Pattern Analysis and Machine Intelligence*, 36, No. 12 (2014), 2483–2509.

Gates, Bill, 'Is There a Crisis in Capitalism?', *GatesNotes*, 20 May 2019. Available at <https://www.gatesnotes.com/Books/The-Future-of-Capitalism>.

Gurovich, Yaron, Yair Hanani, Omri Bar, Guy Nadav, Nicole Fleischer, Dekel Gelbman, Lina Basel-Salmon, Peter M. Krawitz, Susanne B. Kamphausen, Martin Zenker, Lynne M. Bird & Karen W. Gripp, 'Identifying Facial Phenotypes of Genetic Disorders Using Deep Learning', *Nature Medicine*, 25, No. 1 (January 2019), 60–64.

Hagenbeck, Carl, *Beasts and Men: Being Carl Hagenbeck's Experiences for Half a Century Among Wild Animals*, Hugh S.R. Elliot and A.G. Thacker (abridged trans.), London: Longmans Green, and Co., 1912.

Hagendorff, Thilo, 'The Ethics of AI Ethics: An Evaluation of Guidelines', *Minds and Machines*, 30, No. 1 (March 2020). Available at <https://link.springer.com/article/10.1007/s11023-020-09517-8>.

Hankey, Stephanie, Julianne Kerr Morrison and Ravi Naik, 'Data and Age Democracy in the Digital', report by The Constitution Society, London 2018.

Heaven, Will Douglas, 'Predictive Policing Algorithms Are Racist. They Need to Be Dismantled', *MIT Technology Review*, 17 July 2020. Available at <https://www.technologyreview.com/2020/07/17/1005396/predictive-policing-algorithms-racist-dismantled-machine-learning-bias-criminal-justice/>.

Hegel, Georg Wilhelm Friedrich, *The Philosophy of History*, New York: P.F. Collier & Son, 1902.

Hegel, Georg Wilhelm Friedrich, *Lectures on the Philosophy of Religion*, edited by Peter C. Hodgson and J. Michael Stewart, with the assistance of H.S. Harris, Berkeley: University of California Press, 1985.

Hobson, John, *The Eastern Origins of Western Civilisation*, Cambridge: Cambridge University Press, 2004.

Huxley, Alduous, 'A Note on Eugenics', *Vanity Fair*, October 1927. Available at <https://archive.vanityfair.com/article/1927/10/a-note-on-eugenics>.

Jay, Martin, *The Dialectical Imagination: A History of the Frankfurt School and the Institute of Social Research 1923–1950*, London: Heinemann, 1973.

Jernigan, Carter and Behram F.T. Mistree, 'Gaydar: Facebook Friendships Expose Sexual Orientation', *First Monday*, 14, No. 10 (2009). Available at <https://journals.uic.edu/ojs/index.php/fm/article/view/2611>.

Jones, Marc Owen, *Digital Authoritarianism in the Middle East: Deception, Disinformation and Social Media*, London: Hurst 2022.

Jones, T.A., 'The Restoration Gene Pool Concept: Beyond the Native Versus Non-native Debate', *Restoration Ecology*, 11, No. 3, 2003, 281–290.

Kallenborn, Zachary, 'Meet the Future Weapon of Mass Destruction, the Drone Swarm', *Bulletin of the Atomic Scientist*, 5 April 2021. Available at <https://thebulletin.org/2021/04/meet-the-future-weapon-of-mass-destruction-the-drone-swarm>.

Kleinberg, Jon, Jens Ludwig, Sendhil Mullainathan, and Cass R. Sunstein, 'Discrimination in the Age of Algorithms', *Journal of Legal Analysis*, 10 (2018), 113–174.

Kwet, Michael, 'Digital Colonialism: US Empire and the New Imperialism in the Global South', *Race and Class*, 60, No. 4 (2019), 3–26.

Lenin, Vladimir I., *Imperialism: The Highest Stage of Capitalism*, New York: International Publishers, 1939.

Li, Jingwei et. al., 'Cross-ethnicity/Race Generalization Failure of Behavioral Prediction from Resting-state Functional Connectivity', *Science Advances*, 8, No. 11 (2022). Available at < https://www.science.org/doi/10.1126/sciadv.abj1812>.

Lynch, James, 'Iron Net: Digital Repression in the Middle East and North Africa', *European Council on Foreign Relations*, 29 June 2022. Available at <https://ecfr.eu/publication/iron-net-digital-repression-in-the-middle-east-and-north-africa/>.

Madianou, Mirca, 'Nonhuman Humanitarianism: When "AI for Good" Can Be Harmful', *Information, Communication and Society*, 24, No. 6 (2021), 850–868.

Marcuse, Herbert, *One-Dimensional Man*, Boston, MA: Beacon, 1964.

Marcuse, Herbert, *Towards a Critical Theory of Society*, London: Routledge, 2001.

Marino, Mark, 'The Racial Formation of Chatbots', *CLC Web: Comparative Literature and Culture*, 16, No. 5 (2014), 1–11.

'Mark Zuckerberg: Building a Global Community That Works for Everyone', *World Economic Forum*, 17 February 2017. Available at <https://www.weforum.org/agenda/2017/02/mark-zuckerberg-building-a-global-community-that-works-for-everyone/>.

Marx, Karl, 'The Power of Money', in idem., *Economic and Philosophical Manuscripts of 1844*, Moscow: Foreign Languages Publishing House, 1961.

Matz, Sandra, Gideon Nave, and David Stillwell, 'Psychological Targeting as an Effective Approach to Digital Mass Persuasion', *Proceedings of the National Academy of Sciences*, 114, No. 48 (2017), 1–6.

Mill, John Stuart, *Dissertations and Discussions: Political, Philosophical and Historical*, Vol. 3, London: Longmans, Green, Reader, and Dyer, 1867.

Millar, Isabell, *The Psychoanalysis of Artificial Intelligence*, London: Palgrave, 2021.

Neumann, Iver B., *Uses of the Other: 'The East' in European Identity Formation*, Minneapolis: University of Minnesota Press, 1999.

Noble, Safiya Umoja, *Algorithms of Oppression: How Search Engines Reinforce Racism*, New York: New York University Press, 2018.

Nourbakhsh, Illah Reza and Jennifer Keating, *AI and Humanity*, Cambridge, MA: The MIT Press, 2020.

Panagia, Davide, 'The Algorithm Dispositif (Notes towards an Investigation)', *AI Pulse Papers*. Available at <https://aipulse.org/the-algorithm-dispositif-notes-towards-an-investigation/>.

Quijano, Aníbal, 'El estado actual de la investigación social en América Latina', *Revista De Ciencias Sociales*, 3–4 (1988), pp. 159–169.

Rahimi, Babak and David Farid (eds.), *Social Media in Iran: Politics and Society after 2009*, New York: State University of New York Press, 2015.

Rothfels, Nigel, *Savages and Beasts: The Birth of the Modern Zoo*, Baltimore, MD: The Johns Hopkins University Press, 2002.

Russell, Stuart J. and Peter Norvig, *Artificial Intelligence: A Modern Approach*, London: PEV, 2016.

Safranski, Rüdiger, *Nietzsche: A Philosophical Biography*, London: Granta, 2003.

Said, Edward, *Orientalism*, London: Penguin, 1978.

Salgado, José Guadalupe Gandarilla, María Haydeé García-Bravo, Daniel Benzi, 'Two decades of Aníbal Quijano's coloniality of power, Eurocentrism and Latin America,' *Contexto Internacional*, Vol. 43, No. 1 (2021), pp. 199–222

Shiwen Mao, Min Chen and Yunhao Liu, *Mobile Networks and Applications*, 19 (2014), 171–209.

Smith, Adam, *The Wealth of Nations*, Vol. 1, London: Dent, 1910.

Sykes, Mark, *Dar-Ul-Islam: A Record of a Journey Through Ten of the Asiatic Provinces of Turkey*, London: Bickers & Son, 1904.

Tegmark, Max, *Life 3.0: Being Human in the Age of Artificial Intelligence*, London: Allen Lane, 2017.

Tjerk Timan, Maša Galič, and Bert-Jaap Koops, 'Bentham, Deleuze and Beyond: An Overview of Surveillance Theories from the Panopticon to Participation', *Philosophy and Technology*, 30 (2017), 9–37.

Tufekci, Zeyneo, 'Engineering the Public: Big Data, Surveillance and Computational Politics', *First Monday*, 19, No. 7 (2014). Available at <https://firstmonday.org/article/view/4901/4097>.

Van der Veer, Peter, *Imperial Encounters: Religion and Modernity in India and Britain*, Princeton, NJ: Princeton University Press, 2001, 145–146.

Volkova, Svitlana and Yoram Bachrach, 'On Predicting Sociodemographic Traits and Emotions from Communications in Social Networks and Their Implications to Online Self-Disclosure', *Cyberpsychology, Behavior, and Social Networking*, 18, No. 12 (2015), 726–736.

Wang, Yilun and Michal Kosinski, 'Deep Neural Networks Are More Accurate Than Humans at Detecting Sexual Orientation from Facial Images', *Journal of Personality and Social Psychology*, 114, No. 2 (2018), p. 246 (246–257).

Weikart, Richard, 'The Role of Darwinism in Nazi Racial Thought', *German Studies Review*, 36, No. 3 (2013), 537–556.

Young, Robert J.C., 'Colonialism and the Desiring Machine', in Gregory Castle (ed.), *Postcolonial Discourses: An Anthology*, Oxford: Blackwell, 2001.

Zajko, Mike, 'Conservative AI and Social Inequality: Conceptualizing Alternatives to Bias through Social Theory', *AI & Society*, 36, No. 1 (2021), 1047–1056.

Zuboff, Shoshana, *The Age of Surveillance Capitalism: The Fight for a Human Future at the New Frontier of Power*, London: Public Affairs, 2019.

Index